Paths of Former Time

No; no;
It must not be so:
They are the ways we do not go.

Still chew
The kine, and moo
In the meadows we used to wander through;

Still purl
The rivulets and curl
Towards the weirs with a musical swirl;

Haymakers
As in former years
Rake rolls into heaps that the pitchfork rears;

Wheels crack
On the turfy track
The wagon pursues with its toppling pack.

'Why then shun –
Since summer's not done –
All this because of the lack of one?'

Had you been
Sharer of that scene
You would not ask while it bites in keen

Why is it so
We can no more go
By the summer paths we used to know!

Thomas Hardy 1913

From his collection of poems: *'The Darkling Thrush'*

Said to be the Thames Barge 'The Clara,' at the wharf at Battlesbridge (c1922). My uncle John had a half share in this vessel.

Hullbridge School Band, c1937. I am the boy in the front row at the end, on the left as you look at the picture.

Page II

Paths of former time

Tales of farming
and the countryside around Hullbridge
by

John Thorpe

Dedication

*To my wife
Lilian
Who has seen the back of my head
for the past three years while I have
been putting this book together
Thank you Lilian*

I would like to thank all my friends who have been very kind
and helpful to me while I have been putting this
book together, with photographs and memories of some
of the things and happenings that had slipped my memory.

****

To name a few

Jim Worsdale, Len Warren, Edward Hall, Maureen Blake,
Edward Clack, Mary Price and Elizabeth Hardman.

Who have done a lot towards getting this book off the ground.
I thank you all!
And the others I have not mentioned as there have been so many.

****

ISBN 0-9520073-6-3
© John Thorpe

AIRBORNE ART

102 Burnham Road, Hullbridge, Hockley, Essex SS5 6HQ
Tel/Fax: 01702 232823
E mail: spyinthesky@lineone.net

Introduction
Paths of Former Time

I start this story by hear-say from my grandfather and father. We used to sit round the large old kitchen range at Sheepcotes Farm. I listened to them talking about the happenings in the past, since they started farming on their own account.

It starts way back in the late 1800s when the Thorpe's decided to start farming on their own. They came to Hullbridge and bought a small property Hanover Farm, situated on the south side of Lower Road, Hockley. In 1921 they moved to Sheepcotes Farm, which was much bigger and the family, which was growing, wanted more land from which to get a better living.

In the evenings, after the days work was done and we had finished our evening meal, we, that is, granddad, grandma, father, mother and myself would sit round the old kitchen fire. By the light of flickering oil lamps they would talk about the happenings in the past since they started farming on their own, I had nothing else to do but listen and absorb what was said: there were no televisions or

Dick Hymas with wife and son beside the River Crouch.

'wireless sets' in those days to take my mind off the tales which were being told, so I kept all this information in my head, and this is the reason I can write about it now nearly seventy years on.

Although my life did not start until 1929, I think a little should be told about my forebears and their good times and the bad, of how families had to manage on next to nothing; to survive and prosper through sheer hard work, graft and will power. My parents never had it as hard as their parents, and I have certainly not had it as hard as they did. I have had the good luck to be born into the age of great industrial change, and enjoy the benefit of all the machinery on farms today. Also, in all parts of industry technological advances take the very hard work out of life. Whether we are all the better for it, I do not know.

I do hope that parts of this book will enlighten readers about life many years ago on farms and also about other businesses that have had to survive through the many depressions in life. Please forgive me for what I

My Grandfather as a young man.

Page IV

Paths of Former Time

Alice and Agnes at Hanover Farm.

Arthur and Tom Thorpe cutting corn with a one-horse reaper. Aged 13/14, Arthur to be my father in later years.

am going to say now. I think there are a tremendous number of people who have said the same. Although war is not what any of us want, because of all the suffering and death it causes to everyone, it was only the war that put farming back on the map. As most will know, farmers became broke by the hundreds in the thirties and the land went to scrub. Then as soon as war was imminent, millions had to be spent to get the land back into production to feed the nation. The politicians at the time, said war would not happen, but it did and the people suffered.

The many photographs in this introduction show my forebears and others who were involved in farming, before my birth.

Agnes and husband on their wedding day. With her sister May (left), Alice (right) and husband's brother (centre). As you can see, May and Alice in uniform of the First World War. May was made up to a Sergeant Major. She carried out that authority the rest of her life.

Page V

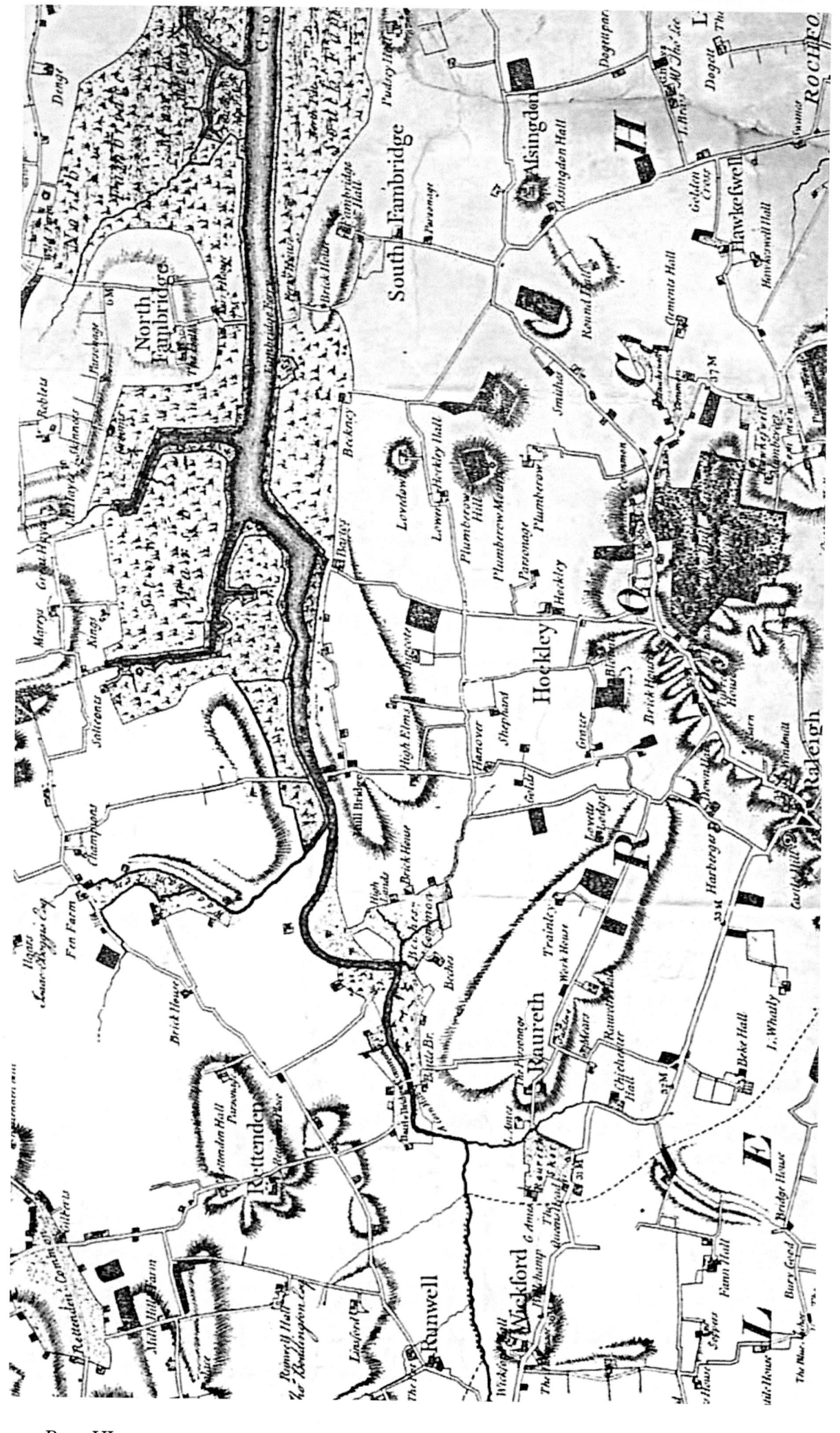

The village of Hullbridge and its environs. With part of the River Crouch. This map is dated 1st September 1777.

Contents

Map of Hullbridge and its environs 1777 ....*Page IV*

Hullbridge and part of the River Crouch, AD 2000..*Page VIII*

The chapters

Chapter 1	John Thorpe; The Very Early Years	*Page 1*
Chapter 2	The School Years	*Page 4*
Chapter 3	At last, school days are over!	*Page 9*
Chapter 4	Walfords and Pollys Farms	*Page 12*
Chapter 5	Earning my keep	*Page 18*
Chapter 6	All work and no play	*Page 20*
Chapter 7	Ploughing and other matters	*Page 26*
Chapter 8	I get the key of the door	*Page 31*
Chapter 9	Disastrous Fire at Walfords	*Page 34*
Chapter 10	Sadness and burdens	*Page 39*
Chapter 11	A fresh clean start	*Page 43*
Chapter 12	Lows and Highs	*Page 45*
Chapter 13	A 'Homemade Car'	*Page 50*
Chapter 14	Hips, Hay and Harvest	*Page 55*
Chapter 15	A Time of Worry	*Page 60*
Chapter 16	A New Start	*Page 63*
Chapter 17	Turning My Hand To Something New	*Page 66*
Chapter 18	More Friends	*Page 69*
Chapter 19	Memories and Friends, Old and New	*Page 73*
Chapter 20	More Friends	*Page 78*
Chapter 21	Yet More Friends	*Page 84*
Chapter 22	Ernie the Higler	*Page 90*
Chapter 23	Life and Hullbridge as it is Now	*Page 92*

Hullbridge and part of the River Crouch

In the millennium year AD 2000

John Thorpe – The Very Early Years

In 1927, Arthur met a young lady, Millie Staines, whose father worked for my grandfather. Arthur and Millie were married late in 1927. Their honeymoon was a half day at Southend, and then back to work, living with grandfather and grandmother. It was not long before grandmother taught Millie to milk the cows. She got on very well with the job. As I think I have said before, grandmother was the driving force, behind the Thorpe Family, and everybody had to 'earn their corn.' Millie became pregnant and I was born on the 17th March, 1929. The doctor who attended my mother was Irish, and because the 17th March was St Patrick's day, he said I should be named Patrick. Grandmother, being a true Scot, exclaimed:

"We're not having that!"

So I was named John after my father, William after my Mother's Father, and George after my paternal grandfather. Henceforth, J W G Thorpe. I have been told that I wanted a lot of attention and looking after when I was a baby, so grandmother and grandfather looked after me, and cooked the meals, and mother went back to milking the cows. As I said, it was all work!

Mother's family was large, seven girls and four boys: they were all hard working people. I think it was said that the boys all worked in the local brick-fields from time to time, but as I heard it, it was more like slave labour. I do remember mothers brother Bill being foreman at a brick-field, off Rectory Road, Rochford, and Jack being head cowman for Rankins, of Great Stambridge, Rochford. After being 'demobbed' from the 1914-18 War, Bert finished his working life with 'Fisons,' the fertiliser manufactures at Bristol. After war work in the second world war, Herbert was a lorry driver, owning his own lorry in later years, carting sand and ballast, for local builders.

Another piece of history told to me by my parents, was that when I was about nine months old, they rented some grass land at Hullbridge along Pooles Lane, for grazing cattle. The cattle that were grazing on this land had to be visited each day, just to see if all was well with them. This particular Sunday evening, they walked from Sheepcotes Farm through the fields to Pooles Lane. Then, after looking at all the cattle and seeing they were

Mother bottle feeding orphan lambs

Sheepcotes Farm House (where I was born)

Page One

John Thorpe – The Very Early Years

OK they went across to the pond to see if there was still enough water for the animals to drink. As they walked past the pond, they looked at each other:

"What's the matter?" father asked.

"I thought I saw an ear above the water," mother replied.

"So did I."

He told mother to wait with me while he went back to have another look. He came back and confirmed what they had seen was true. Father told mother to go back home and he would go to Rayleigh to inform the Police, as that was the nearest Police Station. It turned out to be a man known to them all, George Wright, It was said he tied his hands behind his back and drowned himself. To have done this himself, he must have had a very troubled mind.

It was about this period that father kept a flock of sheep, and sheep as I now know, take a lot of looking after, especially at lambing time, and then its a day and night job. Father and mother used to take it in turns continuously, and through each twenty four hours, until all the sheep had lambed. When you had finished lambing you would have quite a few orphan lambs; my mother and grandmother used to bottle feed them. I can remember them bringing the lambs into the kitchen to warm them up. They would put them close to the large old kitchen range to warm first and then get them to suckle from a bottle, with a mixture of milk and whisky. This would soon revive them. I can just remember these lambs running round the kitchen, as I would be put in my high chair; when all this was going on. I could not stand them running round the kitchen, I was always happy to see the back of them. Those lambs in the kitchen turned me off lamb and mutton meals for a great part of my life.(I only started to eat it in 1995). After they were jumping about they would be put out into a covered enclosure. This was made from hurdles covered with straw, It also protected them from the east winds. And all of these lambs they hand reared, when they had reached the right weight, were sent to Nor Webster to end in his slaughter house in Rayleigh, then sold through his butcher's shop.

Father ploughing at Sheepcotes Farm

Father cutting wheat with tractor & binder with Bert Thomson on the binder

From an early age, as I said, my grandparents looked after me most of the time. I remember riding with my grandfather, in his pony and cart, looking all around Hullbridge, Pooles Lane, and surrounding areas,

Page Two

John Thorpe – The Very Early Years.

for two steers that had become a bit wild, after being let out to graze in the spring. As some animals do for a time until they get used to the bright light. The sheds they were kept in years ago were very dark and when tuned out into the bright light, they ran at a great speed, smashed through the fence and away. It was over a week before they were found.

Word then got to grandfather, that a farmer at Marsh Farm, Woodham Ferrers, had got them in his yard and told him he had seen them swim the River Crouch at high tide: When they got to his side they were exhausted. That was how he was able to get them into his yard, After a couple of days they had settled down, and they were able to get them back to Sheepcotes, and none the worse for their escapade.

It was about this time that the Governor (as grandfather was affectionately known) was having a job to get about, owing to a couple of accidents he had had. One with a bull, and the other with a barn door, he was hit with this barn door during a gale and jammed against the door post. Consequently he was partially crippled. Being around 20 stone in weight, it was a job for him to get about, and he used to go around the farms in a pony and cart; that was after one of the men got him into it.

My mother and father worked very hard, but my father did not enjoy good health, although he kept working. From early in my Father's life and being a good scholar, the Governor made him look after all the business on the farms. This paper work had to be done after he had finished his day's other work.

There was one field on the farm that grew a lot of mushrooms in the season and after mother had finished her morning milking, she would go and pick a bath full (the old fashioned tin bath). Father would take them to a greengrocer in Rayleigh and sell them. In two seasons mother sold £40.00 worth, and started my first bank account.

I think it was about 1930 that my father bought his first tractor,. It was a 'Fordson', grey in colour and made in Ireland. This tractor came from 'Darby's of Wickford,' the local agricultural engineers at that time. This tractor, was a very temperamental thing to start, but once running it would keep going all day and did not get tired like the old horses did: but it did get hot and boil up sometimes. The only thing was, you cooked in the summer and froze in the winter. There was no cab in those days and it had an iron seat,. You had to put a thick sack on it, otherwise you got a sore backside. Apart from all these things the younger generation thought a tractor was a wonderful thing. Father had a drawbar made for the 'McCormick binder'[1] that they had at that time, so they could cut the corn with the tractor instead of horses.

*Three generations of the Thorpes:
Father, The Governor and myself*

[1] A reaping machine that both cuts the corn and ties it into sheaves.

Page Three

The School Years

In 1933 I started school at Hullbridge, about two and a half miles away. By this time father had a car (shared with his brother Tom). I think it was a 'Ford Model T'. Mother and father drove me to school the first day to get me settled in. I did not think much of this, after the freedom of the farms, but had to get on with it! The next day was different, as father had not got the time to run me to school, so one of the horseman's daughters, and one of the other horseman's son's, who were a few years older than me, had to take me, and that meant walking there and home again, and that as soon as possible to do jobs, because grandmother said, everybody had to earn their keep.

The Head Mistress at Hullbridge School at this time was Miss Fasam, and one of the teachers was Mrs Ida Street. When I got home from school, I had to change into older clothes to help with the cows, giving them their rations of feed while they were being milked, and then carrying two pails of water to each cow for them to drink. (There was no main water or drinking bowls[2] at that period). Then I gave them hay for the night. Of course, this procedure was only in the winter, when the weather was too bad for them to be out in the fields.

Sometimes my grandfather would pick me up from school in the pony and cart. This was a lot better than walking! In 1932 Tom's wife Lily, gave birth to a son, Alan Hugh. He was born at Sheepcotes Farm, so my mother could look after her. She went home to Bartons three weeks later. I think that Aunt Lily had her father living with them until he passed away.

Alan started school four years after me, so I had to look after him whilst he was at school, see him home and then do my jobs. Towards the end of 1935 the Governor became ill and after some months of illness, died in 1936. This made things harder for the farming business again. As well as losing a grand old gentleman, there was his will. He had it drawn up so that his four daughters had his share of the Partnership, equally divided between them. Although it only amounted to twelve hundred pounds, this, I can assure you, was a difficult thing to do in those days. But it was done. Grandmother was to be looked after from the farm: again this was done.

At about this time mother had reared fifty ducks. They were getting quite big and mother was telling grandma that some of them were 'going off their legs.'[3] grandma then said:
"They want to be on water, that will cure them."
The next morning mother walked in front of them with a pail of food, and they followed her from the orchard, where they had been kept since they had been hatched, to the pond. When they got there they were soon in the pond, and really enjoying themselves. When it was getting towards evening, father said: "Those ducks should come off the pond, and back in their shed, otherwise the fox will get them."

Hullbridge School as it was when I started in 1934. Headmistress at that time was Miss Fassom. Other teachers were Miss Street and Miss Phillips. The right-hand classroom has been removed to make room for access to the rear of the school where they have built a lot more classrooms, to cope with the growing population and children.

[2] Cattle tested for tuberculosis; known as 'TT' were required to have individual bowls.

[3] A farming phrase to denote that the ducks were ready for the water.

The School Years

We all tried to drive them off, at the shallow end of the pond, but to no avail. In the end father decided that if we drove them all to the shallow end, he would jump in and drive them out. This is what happened, but as I was always at my fathers heels, I jumped in after him. After he had got all the ducks out, he had to jump in again, to get me out: the water only came up to his waist, but it came up to my neck. This frightened me and I began to howl, and that didn't help matters, I can assure you. I was in the 'doghouse' for a few days.

At this time mother and grandma between them kept a lot of poultry, some for laying and some for the table. There would be about six hundred for the table, and mother would kill and pluck these. Father would then take them to Rayleigh. They were sold to Britton, and in turn, he sold them in his fish shop.

When I was about eight years old, and after a lot of pestering, my father bought me my first cartridge shot gun. I had always had an air gun before this, but this was a great step forward. It was a single barrel '410'. I used this for about a year, and then father bought me a double barrel '410'. You can imagine I was well pleased. I used to get one of the cowman's sons who was the same age as me, to go out shooting with me. We often went to the far end of Sheepcotes Farm, and then cross an old lane onto Bartons Farm, where my Uncle Tom farmed. This ran right down to the river.

This area near the river was known as Brandy Hole, and at one time had a house and buildings. There were also a

I have been told this was the whole amount of pupils and Teachers at Hullbridge School in 1937. Left back row: Miss Philips and Mrs Street. Right back row: Miss Lily. In front of Miss Lily is Miss Fasom (Headmistress).

couple of disused wells, and rumour had it, that the smugglers hid their stills and brandy down these. The house and barns had gone by this time, apart from some charred remains. I was told that the farm had burnt down in very suspicious circumstances, so it must have been something to do with smuggling. Anyway, there was a very large pond at the rear, where the house used to stand, and it was surrounded by bushes and trees. It made a good cover for wild ducks, and geese. We were always sure of a couple of ducks or a goose from this pond, and

Page Five

The School Years

often a rabbit, or a hare, then I would sell the hare to a local man, as father and mother didn't like to eat hare. They said it was too strong in taste.

In about 1938 the Governor's brother, John Thorpe, got in touch with my father. He wanted to come and live with us. His wife and son had passed away and he had gone to live with another of his brothers at Grays, but this had not worked out very well. He had been a seaman most of his life, after running away to sea as a very young man. He must have done fairly well for himself, because later in life he owned half share in a barge, named 'Clara,' with A J Meason, who was a very large[4] farmer, who also owned Battlesbridge Mills back around the 1900's. Well father, mother, and grandmother talked it over and decided to give it a trial, bearing in mind they had heard from his brother that he could be very difficult at times. He was a tall man of 6'1, but was crippled and could only walk slowly with two sticks. He was also as 'deaf as a post,' and could barely write his own name, but he came to us. From then on things ran fairly well until 1939, but between 1936 and 1938 a syndicate wanted to purchase, Cracknells Farm, Sheepcotes Farm, Bartons Farm, and land down to 'The Dome' and Wadham Park. The syndicate was known as 'The Kingsmans Park Riverside Estates.' The main man behind this very big project was, Dr Bockasini, an Italian. Land

An after-school chore: Me feeding orphan lambs.

Grandmother and myself at Sheepcotes Farm.

about here, and I suppose in most areas at this time, was valued at around £20.00 per acre. They had very big ideas about the extent of their plans. They proposed to have golf courses, yachting marinas, huge tennis courts, cinemas, theatres, shops and housing estates.

There was also talk that they were going to bridge the River Crouch. But all this was not to be, ('the best laid plans of mice and of men'). The last letter my father had from the syndicate was on 12th July 1938, stating that owing to the international situation, they would have to suspend negotiations for the time being and if things got better, they would resume negotiations. The situation was that the Germans were marching through Czechoslovakia, Poland and there was a threat of war. Anyway, things did get worse; and Dr Bockasini and other foreign nationals were interned; bringing about the end of something that might have changed Hockley and this part of south east England.

[4] In farming terms; a 'large farmer' is one who farms a great deal of land.

Page Six

The School Years

Anyway, farming went on and the threat of war got worse. In 1939 we had a huge fire at Sheepcotes Farm, and lost very big barns, cow sheds, various buildings, hay stacks and straw stacks. This was a very traumatic time for all concerned. As well as losing the feed for the animals, we had no barns to put feed in if we bought more.

I was 10 years old at this time, and it was in September of this year that war was declared; this situation made it very difficult to rebuild the farm buildings. All steel and iron of every description was wanted. Anyone who had iron fences round their premises, such as, schools, parks, large houses, all were confiscated, pulled up and carted away to be melted down to make munitions for the war.

My father had a very good friend, Mr Reg Byford, who was a local builder in Rayleigh. He came to the farm and gave all the necessary estimates for rebuilding the barns and cowsheds. He also helped fill in all the forms connected with getting the

Aunt Lily on one of her many visits to see my mother.

permits to supply steel and timber for the buildings. The new barns came from Wales and by the time the materials arrived it was towards the end of 1940, the men from the factory where they were made, came to erect all the steel work. The men that came worked very hard to get the job finished as soon as possible, so they could get back to Wales. This was because of the air raids day and night. They had not come across these traumatic times in Wales. They managed to get the job done in 'double quick time,' and we were thankful to have barn coverage, and cowsheds once more.

Sometime after this, I was told that Dr Bockansini, with a ship load of other internees was being transported, possibly to Canada, but the ship was torpedoed and everybody on board was lost.

The ducks at Sheepcotes.

The School Years

I think it was about this time that my Uncle Tom came out of Bartons Farm and brought his herd of cows to Sheepcotes. Tom with his wife and son moved into a bungalow adjacent to Bartons Farm. A Mr Eason took on the tenancy of Bartons Farm. Mr Eason had two daughters, Jean and Joyce, who also worked on the farm after leaving school. I think I am right in saying that they had a herd of Jersey cows. We always had a good friendly relationship with the Eason family and still have with the girls. They being around about the same age as myself.

When Uncle Tom gave up Bartons Farm, the Thorpe Partnership had the chance to farm Cracknells Farm, belonging to a Mr Tom Finch, who also owned and resided at Hockley Hall, with his sister and husband, Mr Percy Seed. They remained there for a number of years, before moving to Crown Hill, Rayleigh, a Mr Eddie Baker and his sister bought Hockley Hall from Mr Finch. They moved there from Northlands Farm, High Road Hockley. They were the local livestock and haulage contractors and cattle dealers. Cracknells Farm was not being farmed very well by Mr Finch and the War Agriculture Committee were threatening to take the farm away from him if he did not farm it to its true potential. The Thorpe family was able to lease the farm from Mr Finch and farmed Cracknells to the 'War Ag's' satisfaction. It was only a small farm of about 85 acres and next door to Sheepcotes. Round about this time father decided to change his tractor, and 'went for' another Ford. This came from 'Denoons of Chelmsford,' at this time the local main Ford agents. The old one was sold to a friend of father's, Mr Les Ellis of Merton Drive, Church Road Hockley, who had it stripped down, rebored and painted in its original colour, this continued working for a few years after it was restored. All the work on the tractor was carried out by a local man and a first class mechanic. named George Boul.

Shortly after this father bought another tractor, a 'David Brown Cropmaster.' This was an upgrade on the Ford and red in colour. Both tractors were petrol/paraffin. This means they started up on petrol and when they got warm, you switched over on to paraffin: this was known as 'TVO,'[5] The first winter we had the 'David Brown,' father told one of our men and myself to go and drain the water out of both the tractors, as we were going to have a hard frost. I don't think anti-freeze was used at that time, anyway we seldom used the tractors in the winter. They were on iron wheels, so you couldn't go on the road. We went to the 'Fordson' first, found the tap underneath the radiator, turned it on and drained the water. As we were not familiar with the new tractor, we had to search for a tap. Eventually we found a tap at the bottom of the radiator, turned it on, and looked no further. When we came to use the tractor the following spring, we found to our dismay a cracked cylinder block. By not looking further we had missed a second tap on the block. Father, not being mechanically minded, did not know what to do. He was told that a new engine was the only answer. Father's friend Les Ellis who bought the old Ford, brought George Boul, the local mechanic, up to see the damage. He told us he could repair it, if it could be taken down to his garage at Coventry Corner, Hullbridge. It's odd how some things you can't remember and getting the tractor down to the garage is one of these, however the tractor was taken to George's garage. George soon got to work on repairing the cracked block, after he had done the repairs, he explained how it was done, by drilling holes and tapping a thread and screwing in brass bolts very close together along the crack, from end to end. We had the tractor back and working in less than two weeks, it never leaked again while we still owned the tractor. We had a good bunch of men working for us at this time, horsemen, cowmen and daymen[6]. My mother, father and Uncle Tom were also milking, each person had to milk, nine, or ten cows, night and morning. This was in 1940 and I was now eleven years old and had to go to 'Rayleigh Senior School' until I was 14.

[5] Tractor Vaporising Oil

[6] Daymen worked by the day; not like Horsemen and Cowmen who were employed full time.

Page Eight

At Last – School Days are Over!

I am sorry to say I did not like school, and if I could get out of going, no one was more pleased than me. I would sooner be working on the farm, or ploughing with the tractor, but I was to learn later in life, that I should have stayed at school and gained a better education. But as they say, 'you pays your money, and you takes your choice'.

I learnt to drive a tractor when I was eight years old, and a car at eleven. Going back to the horse-men who my father employed, one man in particular sticks out in my mind more than the others. His name was Charlie Gatward, a good all round man, strong and big built. He kept his horses immaculately. My father purchased two horses for him to work; he bought them both from a Mr John Hollowell, of Coxtie Green, Brentwood, in about 1937. They cost 80 guineas each. Just after Charlie came to work for us, I can remember going with my father one evening to see Charlie and listening to all their yarns, mostly about farming and the surrounding countryside. Charlie had two daughters and two sons. Bob, one of the sons, was looking for a job as a lorry driver. Father had a word with Mr Baker, of Northlands Farm, High Road, Hockley, at this time. After father made the introduction, Bob went to see Mr Baker and got the job. He was with him for a number of years. While Bob was working as livestock haulier with Mr Baker, he met Jean Eason, the farmers daughter of Bartons Farm. Later, Bob and Jean married, I have just been told that they celebrated their Golden Wedding on Saturday, 20th June 1996.

The RAF 'Op's Room' at Blake Hall (c1943). RAF Fighter Command over Essex was controlled from this room when the operations room at North Weald aerodrome was destroyed by enemy action in September 1940.

The crash site of a Heinkel 111. An airman of the RAF Recovery Team examines the propeller protruding from the ground. In the background a soldier stands guard, bayonet fixed and gas mask ready.

Charlie, as I have said, was an all round man. He was a professional man with a scythe; he could cut a lawn with his scythe as clean and level as a cylinder mower. When my father was sick, Charlie would help with the milking. He was always saying that my mother was the hardest working woman he had ever known;

Page Nine

At Last – School Days are Over!

'Blake Hall' near Ongar, Essex. This whole building was taken over by the RAF in 1940 and the 'Op's Room' established in the South Wing (left). Now, still largely as it was it houses the Airscene Museum.

I think he was right: In fact I know he was right.

The war was still going on. They were having bombing raids on London and surrounding areas, both day and night. London was suffering terrible destruction.

Myself when young! Here seen with an 'Empire Star BSA' motorbike.

Being thickly populated the German crews couldn't fail to hit something, not like in the country, where properties were widely spread, but we did have quite a lot of high explosive and incendiary bombs. This was mostly due to our anti-aircraft guns and fighter planes intercepting the bombers; then the raiders just dumped their bombs anywhere and headed back to Germany, unless they were shot down. We had planes fighting overhead some days, to try and stop the bombers from reaching London. This is when they unloaded their deadly cargo 'willy-nilly' and we got them. So you did not know what was coming next.

In late 1940, when my father and his brother had an argument about something or other; it must have been quite an argument because they decided to split the partnership and sell up. Eventually Sheepcotes was put up for sale. It was not one of the best times to sell, but it was put into the hands of a firm of auctioneers and land agents by the name of 'Woodcocks'. It was quite a task to sell at this time owing to the war. Very few farmers had the money or the inclination to buy more land, so it was a long drawn out job.

Page Ten

At Last – School Days are Over!

Anyway, eventually a Major More came along who was interested in the farm for his son. I think this was to keep his son out of the war, although this was odd, with him being a Major in the army. However, after a lot of discussion, they bought the farm. The Mores did not have the farm for more than about three years. Then they sold it on to a Mr Wooltaunton who farmed it for another few years, until he was taken ill, and passed away.

Mr Calab Raynor of the 'War Ag'.

His wife carried on for a while, but I think it got too much for her, so she in turn sold to a Mr Jim Cook.

The Cook family were more interested in cattle farming than arable; anyway, word soon got around that the Thorpe's had sold the farm and a day or two later. Mr Caleb Rayner came to see father, he was not unknown to father, as Mr Rayner and my father had one or two deals together, with Mr Rayner buying growing crops of peas from our farms. Mr Rayner was one of the top men on the 'War Ag' for the Essex area. They had a long talk about what my father was going to do now that he had sold. Father explained that he was contemplating finding a farm in Suffolk and letting Uncle Tom take on Cracknells Farm. However, Mr Rayner had a proposition to put to my father. It was that there were two farms coming up for rent. These were Walfords and Pollys Farms, owned by the Smith family. They were not farming this land as well as they should, and the 'War Ag' were going to take the farms away from them, as they could do when you did not produce the amount of crops the land was capable of in time of war. Well, father spoke to his brother and asked him if he would like to take these farms on himself.

He gave it some thought and came back with the idea, that if my father was to take them on and be the 'Guv'nor', so to speak, then he would certainly go in with him again.

Walfords and Pollys Farms

My father and his brother made arrangements to meet Mr Rayner at Walfords Farm the next day. They walked the farms to discuss the pros and cons of the venture. Both farms were in a very run down state; and everyone could see why they were going to be taken away from the occupiers There were a fair number of grass meadows with their hedges very overgrown and some sixteen feet wide, ditches were clogged up, there was no main water laid onto the fields, only ponds, and not good ones at that. There was one good cowshed to hold twenty cows; that was inadequate for the nearly forty cows that we had at that time, but the brothers had decided to take the farms on.

Now things had to start to happen; firstly to get Reg Byford down to see what could be done to convert existing sheds into cowsheds. This was done by making 'standings' for a further fourteen cows and a shed for the bull. The shed for the bull had to be made strong, with 8 x 2½in. timbers, the door being made of the same material plus heavy iron hinges and door bolts.

The Smiths had a sale of all their implements in mid September. There was no livestock on the farm, except two old horses and we did not want either of these.

So, on September 28th 1942, we moved to Walfords Farm, 'lock, stock and barrel.' Well, it wasn't empty! We found ourselves amongst rats, mice and fleas; the farmhouse was alive with these vermin, and had to be got rid of. We had to have an ambulance to move Uncle John, as we called him.

Grandmother was still going strong doing her daily chores, chopping wood for the fires, (central heating was almost unheard of then) making butter and feeding the chickens; at that time there were between six and seven hundred birds. She was always a hard working woman and couldn't stand anyone who didn't do just that. She would do any job in her power that needed doing, as long as it was helping the business. There was a lot to do to get Walfords into shape as it was so run down and we knew it would not happen overnight. When we moved into the house we only had four rooms available to us, as the Smiths had not managed to move all their possessions out. They had so much stuff and had a job to get it all in the much smaller house at 39 Cambridge Road, Southend, their new home.

In 1942, in winter time and houses had to be 'blacked out' with no light showing at all. We had wooden shutter doors at the front porch that we closed and bolted every night, and all the windows were covered, so that not even a chink of light showed anywhere, so as not to help the Luftwaffe night raiders. It was about seven thirty one evening, when a loud banging came on these front doors. Father went and asked who was there, the reply came: "Would you come out sir, I need your assistance?"

Father would not go outside without his hat and jacket. (His mother had always insisted we all had a hat on when we went out; in winter to keep you warm and summer to keep the sun off of your head). By the time he had done this and gone out of the back door, he saw a torch light coming up the back garden. Father challenged the person.

A shout came back: "Police sir, when I first called you he got away from me but I caught him again down your back garden, could we come inside sir; and have you a phone?"

When they got inside we could see the man was a young soldier. He had been stealing ladies' fur coats. The policeman 'cuffed' (*handcuffed*) the man and while father stood and saw that the man stayed where he was, the policeman went and got all the coats, brought them indoors then rang for a car to come and collect them all.

Walfords Farm house had no main water, no electricity and no gas. It was built in 1900 with two wells at the back. The Smiths had been in the house for 42

Walfords and Pollys Farms

years and never ran out of water. We were there for two weeks and the wells were dry! It was unsafe for the cows to get to the water in the ponds because of the mud, and we lost two cows that did when they got stuck in the ponds. We had to do something quickly. This meant applying for permits to get pipes to lay for main water, and permits did not come easily, it being war time. We wanted 'three-quarter' galvanised pipe, but had to make do with black pipes. These had to be treated with black bitumen both inside and out. We hired a large 'caterpillar tractor'[1] and driver with a 'mole plough,' from the 'War Ag.' This was to pull the pipe through under the ground, so as not to have an open trench down the fields. We had to hand dig a small trench to start and as the tractor went forward you kept screwing the lengths of pipe on.

When all was connected up and water running, we had big blobs of bitumen coming out for a long time, but there, we had water down the fields and in the house.

Although we had main water, we still had to have oil lamps in the house, and lanterns in the cowsheds. We had not got a very good toilet system, only as they used to term it, 'a bucket and chuck it.' We managed to get over the winter of 1942 and into the spring of '43. A lot of fencing had to be done before the cows could be turned out to graze. Owing to other important jobs, such as the laying of the water, we were not able to get any winter corn planted at Pollys Farm, so it had to wait until the next spring and it was then planted with spring barley. Walfords had wheat, mangolds, which are like swedes, for cattle food, potatoes and kale for the cows. Cracknells had wheat, oats, and barley. We also kept the 'in-calf cows,' calves and beef stock there.

As I am mentioning Pollys Farm, I had better tell you how we got the water to the cattle we had turned out to graze at Pollys. There were no ponds of any use for cattle to drink. Father bought three large tanks, and placed one in each of the three grass fields. We used to cart the water there in old seventeen gallon milk churns, there would be six of these churns in a 'tumble cart[2].' We had to go through the fields from Walfords to get to Pollys, as there was no entrance from the Hullbridge Road when the Thorpes started to farm both farms, an entrance was created in much later years. At about this time, Mr Lingood, who ran an old taxi in Rayleigh, was selling the old motor and getting a replacement; you couldn't buy new motors during the war.

This is typical of the pump which would have been used at the farmhouse to supply water, for all the family's needs.

[1] A Caterpillar Tractor is a track laying vehicle; which enables it to traverse most terrains.

[2] A tumble cart can be tipped up in degrees so that varying amounts can be slipped off.

Page Thirteen

Walfords and Pollys Farms

The old car was bought by my father for £8.00, which seemed to be a lot of money at the time. The car was an 'Essex' and in good condition for its age. Father also bought a trailer to tow behind it and we then used it to cart the water to the cattle, instead of horse drawn cart. This old car and trailer served us well for a couple of years, that was until we laid the main water to the farm. We then sold the car and trailer to Mr Johnny Grey, of Hawkwell. I think he paid about fifteen pounds for them, I know he was well pleased with the

advancing and about to overrun his base had to get out of Burma fast. He was coming home and that he had got money to invest. He also stated he wanted to put some money into land. My father told him that he did know where there was a good property which was available, Chichester Hall Farm, Rawreth. A few days later, Ted Devenish got in touch with father again, asking him to make arrangements for them to look over Chichester Hall Farm, as soon as his nephew was home. This was done and a date fixed.

A tractor pulling the mole plough.

deal and drove it for a few years, delivering fencing posts and rails. For that was his business at Hawkwell.

After father and mother had finished the Sunday afternoon milking and had had their tea, they would go for a walk over the farms, firstly to view the crops and secondly for pleasure. Father always carried his shotgun and would usually come home with either a rabbit or pheasant. On one of these Sunday evening strolls he met an old friend, Mr Ted Devenish (the Devenish Family were in the haulage business, chalk, lime etc) They had a long talk, the gist of which was that Ted Devenish had a nephew who was an officer in the RAF and who, because the 'Japs' were

They requested my father to join them to view the farm, Ted Devenish said he valued fathers opinion on farmland.

Chichester Hall Farm was lovely and included a farmhouse and cottage the latter with a moat all the way round. There was also an excellent set of barns and cattle yards, with concrete water troughs in all the yards fed by a windmill pump on the edge of the moat. There were three more cottages by the main road and not too far from the farm. There were approximately 180 acres of good productive arable and grass land. The farm was eventually bought by Mr Webster. (Mr Devenish's nephew) Mr Webster rang father and told him he could go in and

Page Fourteen

Walfords and Pollys Farms

farm Chichester Hall Farm the coming Michaelmas.

My father was rather taken aback and asked why, the answer was: " I do not know anything about farming and you have an excellent reputation. and I can think of no one better to look after my investment." After some discussion, father agreed to take the farm on a seven year lease. Another thing that happened during the war. The Nursery opposite Walfords Farm was owned by Mr Fred Paish and since moving to the farm we had struck up a friendship with the Paishs' and would go down to the 'Anchor' for a drink on Wednesday and Saturday evenings. We would get on a bus and it would take us down to the 'Anchor;' the buses used to turn round in the pub car park. There was a driver and conductor on the buses at this time, and these two were on duty most of the time on these nights, so we got quite friendly with them. When we got to the pub if there was an air raid on, the buses had to stop running.

When this happened the driver and conductor would stop at the 'Anchor' with us; when the all clear sounded, we would all go home. The driver was a keen man with a gun, and because the war was on he could not get many cartridges; but as we were farmers we had a good allocation and father used to let the driver have some so that he could go shooting on his time off. It was rather funny really to see the 'double decker' bus pull up outside the farm and we all got off. Father would then go indoors and get him some cartridges and the bus would continue its journey back to Southend.

Father was very friendly with Mr & Mrs Moss and being farmers we lived a lot better than most. Having a big garden and growing a lot of vegetables: also we had a large milking herd of cows and grew many acres of potatoes, kept chickens, a few turkeys and pigs, so you see we never went short of food. Although we were governed by the 'Ministries of Agriculture Fisheries and Food' and had to be careful of what we did; none the less, we did help a lot of people out (that was on the QT). We often let Mrs Moss have some eggs and butter. Grandma and mother used to

Chichester Hall Farm. Note the moat edged with bullrushes in the foreground.

Walfords and Pollys Farms

make butter all through the war and for a number of years after while we were still on rations. When some of the old chickens had finished laying, they would be killed, plucked and put in the pot and boiled with swedes, carrots and dumplings. This made a very good, cheap meal. We also helped Mr Moss out with some corn for his pigeons (again on the QT). In fact I can tell you now, after sixty years have passed, the local constabulary were not behind in coming to get their bits and pieces also.

We had a young man working with us round about 1942-3, his name was Bert Lord. Bert, his brothers and parents had been known to us for a number of years before we moved to Walfords. The Lord family, were one of the many London families, that had bought plots of farmland on which to build their weekend bungalows. After we had finished work in the summer evenings, we would spend the time catching rats in the brook ditch that ran past the farm. Which, as I said before, was infested with vermin. We tried all sorts of ways to exterminate them; rat traps, poison, gas and guns etc. We succeeded in the end, but it did take about three years.

It was on one of these evenings that Harry Towers, the local greengrocer, came to see my father; we used to supply him with potatoes. He left his old 'Bull-nosed Morris' van parked in the gateway and he had not seen us down in the brook, as we were trying to keep out of his sight. He went through the gate, through the yard, over to the house to see father. After Harry had visited father at the house, Bert said to me: "Let's have a game with him. I'll lift the van up while you put a brick under the axle, so the wheel is just off the ground."

With an old 'Bull-nosed Morris,' with half doors, you had to set the throttle and choke on the steering wheel, switch the ignition on and use a starting handle. When he came back to the car after seeing father, he went through all the procedure, and joy! the engine started.

One of Devenish's chalk spreaders at work.

With a satisfied smile Harry climbed into the driving seat, de-clutched, selected reverse gear and let out the clutch and 'revved' the engine up, but the van didn't move.

He got out of the van, pushed his hat back, scratched his head and walked round the van muttering and swearing

Walfords and Pollys Farms

about motors. He eventually switched the engine off and went back to get my father. During this time we boys got out of the ditch, removed the brick and hid behind the big willow trees. When Harry and father got back, we heard him telling father his gear box 'had gone.' Harry told my father to stand and watch. He then went through all the same procedure again and started the engine.

Back in the van, Harry de-clutched, put the van into gear again, revved the engine and let out the clutch, with a mighty roar the van shot backwards at great speed, right across the road and the driver, had a look of surprise and horror on his face. He managed to stop the motor before he went into the other side ditch. Then he caught sight of us 'laughing our heads off'. Harry, not seeing the joke, jumped out of the van and we took to our heels. He chased us up the road, cursing and shouting what he was going to do to us when he caught us, but we were younger and faster, and he didn't catch us. He 'cooled off' after a couple of weeks, and saw the funny side of the prank.

The Bull Nosed Morris.

Page Seventeen

Earning My Keep

I left school in 1943 and started work on the farm. My first week's wage was five shillings plus my keep. My father said that my keep came to more than my wage!

We had gathered together quite a sizeable piece of land by this time, made up of Cracknells Farm, Walfords Farm, Pollys Farm, Chichester Hall Farm and twenty four acres opposite Bartons Farm. This we rented from the 'War Ag,' I think round about 500 acres in all.

In about the beginning of October 1943, I was ploughing a twelve acre field at Cracknells Farm, down by the River Crouch and when I got home that evening father asked: "Have you finished that field Boy?"

I told him that I had only got to go round the headlands twice more and it would be complete. He then added that I had to be up early next morning to finish the field as there was going to be a lorry there at eight o'clock, to take the tractor and plough to Chichester Hall where it was to start ploughing. I was up 'like a lark' next morning and the field was finished by the time the lorry arrived. By the way the tractor was a 'David Brown' and we loaded it and the plough onto the lorry.

We arrived at Chichester Hall Farm and unloaded the lorry in the farm yard. We had to cross the road to get to arable land, where the farm buildings and house were; the land was all grass.

I went up to the field that I was to plough and the horseman was already at work. He had drawn the field out, making 'heads' every eight feet.

This was going to be put on the 'stetch' for drainage purposes. The next procedure was to take the second furrows off, and then the horseman would put one furrow each way, making the 'stetch' which is eight furrows, four each way.

The horseman my father employed when we took over Chichester Hall, was Sam Wood. He was another 'professional' man with the plough, horse hoeing, corn stacking etc: whatever he turned his hand to, he did well. Later my father made him 'working foreman.'

When 'The Rochford Hundred Ploughing Match' was held, father used to enter his 'corn stacks' in the competition. He mostly came out with first or second place. We also put in mangolds, potatoes, and samples of wheat, oats, barley and a bale of hay. We had a few prizes for these, but it was a job to compete against the Rochford Farmers, mainly because of the type of soil, their soil being much more fertile than ours and easier to work. After we had taken Chichester Hall Farm, I used to help milk in the mornings at home and then go to Chichester Hall after breakfast; that would be at about half past nine and usually I would cycle the four and half miles there.

Most evenings after work father would come over and pick me up, tying the bike on the back of the car to save me biking home and so be fresh for

Corn stacks.

Page Eighteen

Earning My Keep

the early start next day. The old car we had at that time was a 'Flying Standard Twelve,' 1936 model, bought from 'Darbys of Wickford,' in 1939. As it got older, like most of us, it became rather temperamental. By 1943, mainly because it was almost impossible to get spares during the war years. most parts were unobtainable. As a consequence maintenance was almost nonexistent.

After we got 'Chichester Hall Farm we used to send all our 'in-calf cows' there from the other farms until they 'calved down,' then after a couple of days the cows would go back to the milking herd at Walfords, leaving the calves to go onto 'nurse cows.' We had about six of these cows on the farm, as well as a sixty head of beef animals of different ages. Winter time was the hardest work, when we had all the cattle in the yards. They all had to be feed, watered and 'bedded down.' We were always very pleased when spring came around and we could turn the majority of the cattle out to graze.

Uncle John, that is my grandfather's brother, who came to live with us, passed away in 1943. In his will he left my father and mother part of his estate - about £500, and to me he left £84 to be put in trust until I was twenty one. He left another share to a niece.

Round about 1944 we were offered some land that the 'Ministry of Agriculture' had been farming. This consisted of Hanover and Middle Farms, at this time named by the ministry as 'Hockley Garden Estate.' All this land had been 'let go' and became derelict from about 1921 when my grandfather sold it.

I can remember, as a lad, walking about the fields, or should I say wilderness, because the bushes and trees had grown to look like a 'young forest,' As soon as war was imminent, and the 'War Ag' was formed, they put gangs of men and all the tractors and winches that they could muster up to clear vast areas of land ready for food production once again.

Hanover and Middle Farms were not the only places that needed attention, a few of the others I knew about were, Lower Hockley Hall, Trenders Hall, Downhall and they were just around this area. There were thousands of acres to be brought back into production.

They eventually got it cleared and had a few crops from it, and then tried to pass it over to one of the local farmers. Anyway there was something like 160 acres of land, and not the best of land at that, but we accepted a lease on it. We had some good crops and some bad. And as always, we kept 'at it,' sometimes when the weather was against us it was heart-breaking, but when the weather was with us, it was a pleasure.

We used to grow about 36 acres of potatoes a year, spread over all the farms at that time. Mostly 'King Edwards,' 'Red King' and 'Majestic.' The yield before grading was on average, 9-10 ton an acre, but Chichester Hall did much better often yielding 12 tons of 'Red King' and 14 of 'Majestic' per acre.

When the potatoes were lifted they were all 'clamped' in the open. Firstly the heaps were covered with wheat straw, and then it was all covered with earth about eight inches thick to protect the potatoes against frost.

Well I have been on about work most of the time, but as I remember that is what life was all about years ago, on the farm anyway!

Father's car, a 'Standard Flying 12.'

All Work and No Play

I will now tell you a little of what we did on Saturday and Sunday evenings.

We used to get finished milking at five o'clock on Saturday and Sunday evenings as we were allowed to start milking a quarter of an hour earlier than normal. One of the lads who worked on the farm with us, was Charlie Newman. So it was that Charlie, Boba Wood, Brian Leeks and one or two others would all catch a bus, and go either to Rayleigh, Hadleigh, or Southend, to the 'pictures.' Or sometimes, in the summer, to the 'Kursaal,' which was a huge amusement park in Southend. I must say before I go any further, that I had not been to the 'pictures' at all before I left school at 14. I did once have the chance to go, but was taken ill and missed it. I will tell you the reason, during the war when I was thirteen, we had a 'waste paper drive' at Rayleigh Senior School, and the class that collected the most waste paper in one week were to win free tickets to the 'Rayleigh Regal,' the local cinema. At the end of the 'drive', classses 2A and 2B drew in the competition, so we all got tickets for a Saturday morning show. But I could not go and I have told you why.

Well as I said, we all used to go out together, and we thought we were 'the lads.' All dressed up in our 'Sunday best,' mostly alike, in dark suits, white shirts which had a changeable collar with starched long points, a white silk scarf and black shoes. We didn't give any bother to anybody, we just had a good time.

But I must tell you about the time we were in Southend at the 'Kursaal.' We had all spent too much money on the different amusements and didn't have enough money for the fare home to Rayleigh. We walked from the 'Kursaal' to Victoria Railway Station, bought a 'tupn'y' (two penny) platform ticket and waited until the train was pulling out of the station and then we all jumped on board. When we got to Hambro Hill, that is just before Rayleigh Railway Station, one of us pulled the communication cord, and when the

Loading the haywagon. My cousins on holiday at the farm look on.

Page Twenty

All Work and No Play

train had slowed down enough we jumped off and ran down the embankment, then onto the road and home.

We had some good times together in the evenings after work. Charlie and Boba had a couple of old motor bikes we used to mess about with. And the motor bikes, being old, meant we were always tinkering with them to get them going. I think we spent more time trying to start the bikes than we did riding on them. These bikes were not licensed, so we rode them on the fields and had some good fun.

During haymaking and harvest there was no time for pleasure. We did not worry though because we enjoyed our work. Haymaking was still being done by cutting with a 'five foot cut, finger mower,'[1] either pulled by horses or tractor. After cutting the hay would be left to 'lay to make' for a couple of days, then turned and left for another two or three days, then it would be put into rows with horse and rake. After this a gang of men would then 'fork it' into 'haycocks'[2] which were left in the field for about a week to ten days.

After that the hay was loaded on to a horse and wagon, carted back to the farm-yard and stacked, close and handy, for feeding the animals in the winter.

A McCormick power binder, sheaves and traves.

It was when I was about fifteen, and 'still a bit green,' when we were haymaking at Walfords. The two horsemen at that time were Charlie Gatward and Bob Steward. It was always done that the horseman loaded his own wagon. All I wanted to do was to load a load of hay. After a lot of persuading, the horsemen decided to let me have a go. Then I found out what it was like to load hay; they forked it up to me on the wagon, in such large fork fulls that I had a job to stand up, let alone pile the hay. Anyway, at last we got loaded, roped on and set off to the farm. Going through the gateway was a bit rough and the load fell off, I cannot print what was said to me. We got the ropes untangled and both men climbed onto the wagon and said: "Right boy, we pitched it up once, now it's your turn."

What '******' hard work it was! They gave no quarter and taught me a lesson I've never forgotten. I was not yet a man, and it was a few years before I had any sort of wagon to load again, and that was when it came to the corn harvest time once more.

We had upgraded our binders from 'five foot cut McCormick land drive,' to 'eight foot cut Massy Harris,' and 'McCormick International power binders.'

The corn was cut and the sheaves were standing in rows. These rows were called 'traves' or 'stooks,' depending on which part of the country you came from. The corn stood in the 'stooks' until it had dried out, then it was carted to where ever you wanted to stack it.

Some farmers would stack it in the field where it had grown; this was so they did not have to cart it too far and that saved time.

---

[1] *This had five finger like projections forward which gathered the hay into bunches for cutting*

[2] *As the heaps were called.*

All Work and No Play

The only drawback to that was getting the threshing machine to the stacks when it was needed, often in the winter. After the hay and corn stacks were made, to finish them, they had to be thatched to keep them dry until such time as they were wanted for use.

The thatcher's name was Dober Shelley of Greensward Lane, Hockley. He had a few sons who used to help him from time to time. Dober was a very nice old gentleman, but he was a hard task master as a younger man. His sons in turn left him for other jobs However, as he got older he mellowed and his last and youngest son, Stan, stayed with him until the end.

Dober had a big house in Greensward Lane with a very large garden; more than an acre. The garden was 'hand dug' then, which was hard and intensive work. In it he grew the most wonderful crops that you ever did see; onions, carrots, beet, potatoes, marrows; you name it, he grew it!

When Dober passed away, Stan carried on the family business of thatching, and Stan's eldest son, Steve followed in his father's footsteps, although there was less and less stacks to thatch, owing to change in farming practice, Stan and his son went into thatching houses. Sadly, Stan had a very bad attack of asthma and passed away shortly afterwards. Steve is still doing a 'professional' job thatching houses today.

Three generations of 'thatchers': Dober Shelley is on the left, his son Stan is next to him And Stan's son Steve is almost hidden under a load of wheat straw. Inset: Steve still carries on the family tradition, he is seen here thatching a house.

While I am talking about the Shelleys, I am reminded about rabbiting. From an early age I was always keen with a gun and used to pester the life out of Dober to come shooting and ferreting on the farms most Sundays.

This he and his brother Jack would do when Jack was on leave from the Navy. We had some wonderful sport in those days, right up until Dober got too old to go out. I treasure the memories.

Page Twenty Two

All Work and No Play

The war was still going on and we had an army camp about one and half miles away, so we saw a lot of coming and going of the army. Also, as I have said, we were under one of the flight paths to London, so we saw a lot of German bombers going over. Some unloaded their bombs when they were intercepted by our fighters. If I remember rightly, it was about this time that the Germans started to send over the 'doodlebugs.' (the 'V1 flying bomb'). They used to frighten us a great deal because you never knew where they were going to fall out of the sky. I can remember one coming over about nine o'clock one morning and my poor old grandmother saying: "Old Mrs Smith is making a funny noise this morning," She had heard us talking about 'Messerschmits.'[3]

The 'doodlebug' engine cut out and it crashed on Woodham Ferrers railway line and exploded. Grandma exclaimed: "I told you it was not working right!" She was eighty one at that time.

Whilst the war was on, and after for that matter, everyone had difficulty in obtaining new farm machinery and had to apply to the 'War Ag' to get whatever piece of machinery they wanted. Britain was importing tractors and machinery from America and the 'War Ag' then distributed the imports to the farmers who were in most need.

If there was a farm sale, and there was some nearly new machinery that a few farmers wanted, you were asked to write your name on a 'ten bob[4] note.' These were put into a hat and who-ever's name was pulled out could buy that piece of machinery at the new price. The remaining money in the hat went to charity. We had put our name down for a new tractor with the 'War Ag,' it was a 'Case LA,' noted to be one of the best 'wheeled tractors' of that period. It was a good ploughing tractor and also drove a 'threshing drum.' We had been waiting a very long time to get this tractor, for it was being imported from the USA, as was a lot of other farm machinery, but nothing had come to light as to when we were going to get our tractor. By this time the war with Germany had finished. The army camp that I previously mentioned was now filled to capacity with German POWs.[5] A lot of these were put to work on farms and on threshing machines. We had three working for us for about two months, haymaking and grading potatoes and we found them good working men. Two of the men spoke good English and told us they did not want war; but as you know, when the law of the country calls, you have to comply, whether you like it or not. I think that most of our men who had to go to war, would have told you the same.

A replica of the doodlebug: The German 'V1' flying bomb. Here seen 'flying' in the RAF operations room at Blake Hall which was dedicated to destroying it. Inset: Part of the RAF operation's board. at Blake Hall. The RAF called doodlebugs 'divers,' this shows that on 31 January 1945, 24 'divers' were destroyed.

[3] The 'Messerschmit 109' was a classic German fighter aircraft of WW2.

[4] Shilling.

[5] Prisoner's of war.

Page Twenty Three

All Work and No Play

Well, as I said, the war was over, and things were looking a lot better, so much so, that West Hanningfield organised, and put on a small 'Agricultural Show.'

Somehow or other agricultural machinery dealers got a lot of implements and tractors together and were touting for trade, most was second-hand. One of these traders was James Barr of Sandon Garage,' near Chelmsford. He introduced the 'Field Marshall Tractor' to this part of England at this show. Three people bought these tractors as a result. One was Mr Percy Baker of Rawreth Hall Farm, another was Mr George Keeling of Crays Hill, Billericay, a threshing contractor, and the third was ourselves.

The tractor was powered with a single cylinder diesel engine and mounted on rubber tyres. It could be started by cartridge, or with a starting handle, but you needed two men on the handle. Well, you could exclaim: "Sods law!"

Because a fortnight later we had a letter from the 'War Ag' stating that the tractor we had been allocated was now ready for delivery. My father wrote back to them saying that we were all right for tractors now, explaining that he had bought the 'Marshall.' They were not offended, as they had plenty of takers for new tractors. By the way, we traded the old; 'David Brown' in against the 'Marshall,' the Marshall being about seven hundred pounds, I can't remember what we were allowed on the 'David Brown.' We had other tractors then, an old '10/20 International,' a standard 'Ford' and also a 'Fordson Major.' The later was powered with a Perkins Diesel engine and was on rubber tyres, but not a good tractor on 'rubbers,' although very handy on the road, especially as the farms were spread about.

I remember we put drawbars onto two of the 'horse wagons' then we could pull them with tractors. This made a lot of difference to carting our produce about. However, eventually we bought two 'four wheel trailers,' known as the 'North Stoke Wagon.' These made another big improvement in moving the produce. Potatoes from the field to the 'clamp,' carting corn, hay, straw and mangolds, as by this time we were producing a lot of these crops.

We also had a lot of cattle, and where there are cows calves follow, which together with the beef stock, created work for seven days a week. I think that when we had finished the 1946 harvest of hay and corn and had lifted the potatoes: it proved not a bad year. But then we had to get on with the ploughing and get ready to plant wheat, oats, barley and pull and clamp the mangold. Coming onto winter the cows had to be kept in and this makes a lot of extra work, but it had to be done.

Quite a few years before this, I think about 1920-21, father had a coal and coke business, delivering to people in Hockley and Hullbridge. He sold the coal business to Les Ellis, who in turn sold to Morris Ilsley.

In the winter, all the grass roads in Hullbridge were impassable with a lorry in the first instance so Morris used to hire a horse and cart with a driver to get the fuel to the householders. These properties were built between 1920 and the start of WW2 in 1939. This was the period when farming was at its lowest ebb.

Local developers bought up some of this land, bearing in mind land was only about twenty pounds an acre then, so I have been told. They would put up a marquee, advertise in the London newspapers inviting

A 'Messerschmit 109' of the Luftwaffe.

Page Twenty Four

All Work and No Play

families down for the weekend. The visitors would be given a few drinks to 'soften them up' before trying to sell them a plot of land. The cost of one plot would be about five pounds: if the person was 'well breached,' to coin my grandmother's phrase, they would possibly buy two or three plots, the plots being twenty feet wide and about two hundred feet deep.

I don't think planning permission was required at that time, so they built their simple 'weekend shacks' on their plots and came down most weekends throughout the summer.

Some of the people who came to Hullbridge initially to buy a plot had a bit too much to drink, and when they came back to take over their land they didn't know where to find it. Even today some of these 'lost plots' can be seen in the village.

There were other places besides Hullbridge that sold land off in plots. To name a few, Woodham Ferrers, Laindon, Ashingdon and I suppose in many other parts of the country. Up until about ten years ago, I have heard that descendants of the people who bought plots all those years ago, are still trying to find them; but I know that they stood no chance. For the 'Land Commission' compulsory purchased most of them, so the land would not go back to the terrible state it was in the twenties and thirties.

Grasmere Avenue, Hullbridge as it was in 1928.

When war broke out, and the bombing started in London, lots of families lost their homes. Some of these owned a weekend place in Hullbridge, and at the other places I have mentioned, had no other choice but to move into them permanently. They would then commute to London each day to their places of work, then home again at night. The early morning buses used to be packed full taking the people to Rayleigh Railway Station, then by train on to London. This was why we came to be carting coal to all these small dwellings; and some were not so small.

Most of the families that moved down to Hullbridge never returned to London to live after the war. They seemed to like it here, so they stayed on, and brought up their families here. There were still no made up roads, so we were still carting coal in the winter long after the war was over, but doing the job with tractor and trailer. This job came on the first Monday of each month, throughout the winter. Morris and his men used to load both lorries on the Saturday to be ready for the Monday morning delivery. We always started at Burnham Road, going onto Hilltop Avenue, Crouch Avenue, Hillcrest Avenue, and so on. One man, I remember in particular, was Trish Shelley, he went to work for Morris after he was demobbed from the army. He was used to a bit of rough work, considering he had come through Dunkirk and other battles. It was mostly my job with the tractor, so this is how I came to work with this man, although we had known each other most of our lives. Him being one of the sons of Dober Shelley, who did all our thatching for years.

In one day's coal humping we would deliver seventeen and a half tons, a '******' good day's work by anybody's standard. On those days, it mostly rained, I don't know why, but it did! I remember getting home one wet day, after carting coal, black water was dripping out of the backside of my trousers, but that didn't worry me too much, because Morris had given me ten shillings extra; at that time a big tip. Mother was not so happy, had a good moan, and told me I had ruined five pounds worth of clothes.

Page Twenty Five

Ploughing and Other Matters

We got Christmas over and into 1947. In March 1947, grandmother passed away after a short illness. Now, bearing in mind that grandma had had a healthy life and also a hard working one and was doing her bit until the end, her death was a great loss to the Thorpe family. She was always there for you with friendly and sound advice, she was 84 when she passed away. 1947 was a bad winter. It started to freeze in February and continued right up until May, with wind frosts as well as ground frosts. It was a blessing when it did break and the weather warmed up. When you get all these adverse weather conditions in farming it puts everything behind. I know you will hear people say:

"Don't worry, they will all catch up," but I have yet to see the yield as good as in a normal year.

In the autumn of 1947, I was ploughing at Pollys Farm, it was about seven o'clock in the evening. When father came to see how I was progressing, he had met Mr Jim Pinkerton, (a neighbouring farmer) on his way to see me. The Pinkertons had been friends of the family for years. I think the reason for them being friends was that Jim's father and my grandmother were Scots. Anyway, when Jim saw my ploughing, he said that I should be put into the Rochford Hundred Ploughing Match. I told him I didn't want to go in with a three furrow plough. He came back with:

"You can borrow my 'Lister Cockshutt Four Furrow."

I could see that between them, I couldn't get out of going, I had his plough for a couple of days before the match to get used to it.

So on the Saturday I went to the match. The match was held at Rochford on Doggetts Farm, belonging to Mr Warren Squires. I made a nice job of my ploughing and was commended, but I won no prize. The reason being the minimum depth was six inches and I had only ploughed four inches deep. The next year the match was held at Rochford, but this time at Rochford Hall Farm which was farmed by Mr Cecil Hurst, an excellent farmer. Father had bought me a new plough by this time, it was a 'Fisher Humphries Four Furrow.' So once again, off to the match I went. I must say I was a bit apprehensive after the year before, but I was told, you never got anything if you don't try. I got to the match and met a lot of other tractor drivers whom I knew. One in particular was Jack Whitbread who worked on the farm that we were ploughing. Jack was a 'tip top' ploughman, and I was ploughing against him. I did not stand a 'snowball's chance in hell.' But I was there and got on with the job in hand. As it happened, I made a fair job of my work and much to my surprise, I came away with first prize. I got second and third prizes in '49, 50 and 51. Then in '52, I won first again and also gained first for the straightest furrow.

When you get a first at a local match, it makes you eligible to enter the County Championship Match at Chelmsford on the following Saturday. Because we were a long way away we had to get the tractor and plough there on the Friday evening before the match so as to be ready to start early Saturday morning. Well once again, 'lady luck' smiled on me and I came third in my class. I was pleased because there were forty six in the class.

We had got through '47 and into '48, when things seemed to be getting better all round, while gradually getting over the war. I understood they were

The River Crouch at Hullbridge frozen over in the winter of '47.

Page Twenty Six

Ploughing and Other Matters

trying to rebuild London and other places that had terrible bomb damage during the bombing. For a couple of years before 1958 my cousin's son Michael, had come to spend his summer holidays with us. He liked it so much that he wanted to come to live with us and work on the farm when he left school.

This was agreed with the parents, and Michael came to live with us in about July 1958. He started in the cowshed, feeding the cows while they were being milked, carrying the milk to the dairy to be cooled, helping my mother to hand feed calves, as she always did this job as well as milking her eight to ten cows. After a few years Michael started courting Stella, a young lady from Rawreth. Eventually they decided to get married and wanted somewhere to live, so we bought a large caravan for them and got permission to site it on our land opposite Walfords Farm. Michael and Stella moved in and were there for a few years; both of their children were born there and Christened Clare and Mark. After a while they managed to get a Council House in Hockley as there wasn't enough room in the caravan for the now larger family. Michael got a job at Fords tractor plant in Basildon, until 1999 when he was made redundant. He now has a job at Woodham Ferrers, he comes and helps in our garden at weekends and is a real asset to us now we are both over seventy years old.

I cannot remember the exact year when they started to knock down the air raid shelters in this area, but when they did, they wanted it all cleared, so anybody could have the rubble for the taking. I should say we collected thousands of yards of brick rubble. It was not an easy job as large sections were joined together with iron reinforcing rods, put there to make it bomb resistant. But, nevertheless we had it to make up the yards and gateways, round the drinking troughs, and also to make the road up to Cracknells Farm. This road had taken a hammering when the army had six or seven gun emplacements on the eastern side of the road leading to the farm. Not many people would remember them being there; until we made the road up it was almost impassable with deep ruts made by the big four wheel drive lorries that pulled the large guns into place. Also when the steam threshing machine had to get to the farm, they always made a mess wherever they went, as it was always in the winter when they came to thresh your stacks of corn.

It was whilst I was carting this brick rubble that I had an accident with my tractor and trailer. I was coming home to Walfords Farm with a large load, I had the choice of two ways from Rayleigh, and decided to take the one that went down Hambro Hill. Ernie Wood, the foreman's son from Chichester Hall Farm who worked for us then, chose to go along the road further and go down Hockley Church Hill, as he was going to Cracknells Farm with his load. Now Hambro Hill is one of the steepest hills around this way and it was raining fast, making the roads very slippery.

The hill has a bend at its steepest point and it was here that the trailer pushed the tractor sideways turning it upside down and stripping the front carriage off the trailer I myself was very lucky. Although I was under the tractor, I only had a lump cut out of my head and bad bruising to my collar-bone. After that escapade, as you might guess, we have avoided coming down that hill with a load again. Ernie told me later that day that his load had pushed him into a skid, but as luck would have it, he managed to control it. After he had got his rubble unloaded, he had to come and help us clear the road of my load, it was very late that night when we finished. I don't think I had better put in print what my father called me for even attempting to come down Hambro Hill with the very large load I had on.

In about the winter of 1951 we had a very heavy fall of snow, the Nursery owned by Miss Wright and close to Pollys Farm had about two acres of glass, all under one roof and they had no heat in them then. The snow was so wet and heavy that all the greenhouses collapsed, putting Miss Wright in money troubles. Miss Wright owned ten acres of land between Hullbridge Road and Pollys Farm, this piece of land father would have liked to

Page Twenty Seven

Ploughing and Other Matters

purchase. After a few months Miss Wright offered this field to father and after some negotiation he bought the field. By purchasing this piece of land, it gave us easy access to Pollys Farm, something we had not had since taking over the farms in 1942. Father had a track made up to the farm with brick rubble and topped with clinker, the clinker came from the Southend gas works.

Ernie and myself, would start off at six o'clock in the morning, to go and get the clinker, bearing in mind the tractor's top speed was only six mph, when we got there it was all hand shovelling to load, so it was an all-day job. After the track was finished it made it a lot easier to get threshing machine, lorries and farm implements to the land.

Sometime after this purchase was made, another twenty four acre field came onto the market. This was named Glaziers, many years ago it was a small farm and still kept its name. Now as it happened we held the

Cracknells Farm, note the road to the right which was reinforced with rubble from the air raid shelters and was also the road which led to the gun emplacements.

Ernie Wood at Chichester Hall Farm. Rawreth, note the tall windmill in the background.

Ploughing and Other Matters

only way to this field, this being the track that we had made to Pollys Farm. My father later bought Glaziers, and put the two pieces of land together, and invested it in my cousins and my names, those being, John and Alan Thorpe.

"So now," said father, "the boys have got some land."

Farming was going fairly well, we had some good crops and some not so good, father had a saying, 'that if everything you did was to turn out well, you would get too well off for your own good.'

We used to grow a lot of hay to feed to our stock in winter. If we had a mild winter and we had a lot left over, then we would sell the surplus to various forage merchants. Years ago, the local thatcher was also, what was termed 'a hay tyer.' He would cut the hay out into oblong shapes with a special hay knife and then put it into a press and tie it with three strong strings at intervals along the bundle. These were called 'trusses' and I think forty eight 'trusses' went to a load. In later years we had it baled with a 'stationary baler,' these were big bales weighing about one hundredweight each, these were very heavy to handle.

We also used this method in the fields, by placing the baler in the middle of the field and sweeping the hay to it with a 'hay sweep.' The hay sweep was about fourteen feet wide, with long wooden prongs, steel-tipped, and was fixed to the front of a tractor. Then it would push large heaps of hay to the baler. This was a lot quicker than carting and stacking, but you had to have good dry sunny weather.

After a time they brought out the 'pickup baler.' This machine was towed by a tractor and could be driven by power shaft from the tractor, while some 'pick up balers' were built with their own stationary engine on them. Our first baler was one of these, an 'International 50T,' powered with an 'Armstrong Sidley' twin cylinder diesel engine. It was slightly bigger than its rival, the 'Massy Harris.' As these were bigger, the bales were a

Hay cutting, how it was done many years ago, note the special hay-cutting knife can be seen towards the left at the top of the picture.

job for two men to pitch onto a trailer with a fork, so we bought a 'Lister Blackstone' multi level elevator. This made life a lot easier. But you still had to have good weather. This you couldn't buy!

The farming world was changing fast. New and bigger tractors, ploughs, rotavators, spring tine cultivators, rolls, sprayers and all manner of machinery, because now the war was over, the factories that made war weapons, were turning their skills into other fields. Machinery dealers were pressurising all the farmers to buy, but farmers have long memories and are a wary bunch. They do not forget the hardships of the' 20s and '30s, so are reluctant to get into debt by buying new tackle.

The Government in that period were promising not to let farming go back to what it was in those inter war years. But we all know what politicians are like. I think at this time the Government was calling for more production from the land, to make England more self sufficient. They were offering good subsidies for land drainage, and a lot of farmers did take advantage of them. Once the land was 'tile and mole drained,' it most certainly paid for itself in a few years. The other advantage it had was that you were able to do away with putting the land 'on the stetch' and also do away with 'water furrows' and plough the land on the flat. This made things better, especially when the 'combines' came

Ploughing and Other Matters

Sam Wood at work with his horses.

along. It was remarkable how this drainage worked on some of the fields that we had drained.

Time journeys on Spring, Summer, Autumn, Winter, Sunrise Sunset; they all come and go, some good, some bad. Life on the farm is changing, so much so that you don't have as many men working on the land. This is because of, as they say, progress. I think the main progress is in tractors, ploughs, combine harvesters and all the other implements that are now on farms at this time.

I look back in my short lifetime to when a horseman went into a field at seven o'clock in the morning to start ploughing, bearing in mind that he had been up two hours earlier to feed, clean and harness his horses for the day's work. He would take nosebags for his horses 'dinner' and possibly bread and cheese for himself. After he had ploughed the one acre that was his day's work; and quite hard work at that!

In about 1950 a man and a medium sized tractor with a two furrow plough would have ploughed five or six acres. It speaks for itself why men were leaving the land. The Ministry of Agriculture were still offering ploughing grants, for farmers to plough up some more of their grass land and bring it into food production, as the country was still short of food. We did plough up some of Pollys Farm at this time, also the land known as Glaziers that we had bought. This land had a lot of large elm trees round it and father sold these to 'John Sadd & Sons' of Maldon. We had an offer of three pounds per tree from another firm. (that was for sixteen trees,) Sadds offer was £425.00 for the same number of trees, subject to the Forestry Commission's OK.

I get the Key of the Door

In March 1950, I became twenty one and the money that Uncle John had left in trust for me until I came of age was duly paid. It had grown from £84.00 to £148.00 and father said to me :

"Well boy, you have always been on about a milking machine, now you can buy one."

So I bought an 'Alfa Laval 3 unit machine,' a 'Lister; one and half horsepower petrol engine with a pump and had all the cowsheds 'piped out.' The total cost was £140.00 and all was installed by 'Darby's of Wickford.'

In and around the '50s we were getting our herd of cows over to 'Red Poll' cows (these were cows without horns) so that when we 'yarded' them in the winter, they did not damage themselves. Also at about this time we were told that if we wanted to stay in the milking business, the herd would have to be 'Tuberculin Tested. This meant having a 'T.T.' test. This we had done and only six cows and the bull passed, so after a lot of discussion, we decided to sell the lot and start afresh. This was only at Walfords, the cattle at Cracknells and Chichester Hall all passed the test without any trouble. We had to change all cowsheds from wooden stalls, to either steel or concrete, so we decided on concrete. These were cast by Mr Reg Byford at his yard in Rayleigh, duly delivered and erected in the sheds. Also at this time drinking bowls, another 'T.T.' requirement, were installed.

There was a time limit to get back into milk production again, so something had to be done fairly soon as we had only three weeks to complete the requirements, otherwise we lost 'four pence halfpenny' per gallon for the milk.

We saw an advertisement in the 'Essex Weekly' for a herd of 20 cows of mixed breeds they were all in calf. My father was not too well at the time, but as time was running short, father his brother and myself, drove to 'Steeple marshes,' right down by the water, to look at the cows. It was typical coastal salting and marsh country and as bleak as I had ever known. We looked at the herd and saw them being milked. I personally was not impressed at what I saw, maybe because of the weather. On the way home father and his brother talked it over

Myself with my two cousins at the front door.

Page Thirty One

I get the key of the door

and decided to sleep on it. Nothing was done for a couple of days and father got rather upset. He said that if we did not 'wake our ideas up' we would lose the extra money for the milk. So he ordered me and his brother to go down to Steeple on the Friday morning to see the cows being milked and if they yielded the amount of milk stated, then we were to buy the herd of twenty cows for £1400.00, that done, we arranged to have them brought home to Walfords as soon as possible. We carried out my father's orders and the cows were delivered the following week, by this time one of the cows had calved, so 21 animals came. These cows did us well and we added to the herd until we had about 55 cows in milk production, with an average of 230 250 gallons of milk a day; and it all bore the 'TT' label.

A cow herd at Walfords Farm.

It was about the same time that I bought a 2 KW generator and we had the house and buildings 'wired out' for electricity. The generator had a 6 hp Jap petrol engine on it. This used too much petrol, so we bought a new Lister six hp diesel engine and put it on the generator. This was very economical to run, we ran this for about 18 months until the generator was nearly worn out, then we negotiated with the Electricity Company to lay the mains on. We had the 11,000 volt line running through the farm about half a mile away and after some haggling they agreed to lay it on for £800.00, the main cost being the transformer, this device reduced the power down to 230 volts.

This was followed with another piece of progress. The next job we tackled was to lay the water on to Pollys farm, again. This had been done about eight years before, in black pipe, not galvanised. Something in the soil corroded it and we had 'everlasting' burst pipes. Permission was needed from the Water Board to use plastic, as at that time plastic was relatively untried, and they did not like you to use it. The meter had to be at the start of the supply, so as to make us responsible for any loss of water due to leaks.

In about 1956 we were negotiating with a Mr Goymer of Muggeradges Farm, Battlesbridge, to purchase 40 acres of land that he owned at Rawreth, adjoining Chichester Hall. This land was two 20 acre fields, the first field next to the main road was arable, the bottom 20 acres was down to grass. At the bottom of the grass field is a very big brook ditch, that runs into the River Crouch, and it is tidal. This means that when the tide comes in it holds the ditch water back and sometimes the brook fills to capacity.

Anyway, we bought the 40 acres and it was a good productive piece of land. The twenty acres of grass land was laid very wet but we grazed it for a few years and then we had it 'tile and mole' drained. After this was done we decided to plough it up and try some wheat in it, I don't think this land had had arable crops on it for the previous fifty years or more. So when we got our first crop of wheat we were more than pleased. The drainage was a lot to do with it as well.

The year 1957 proved to be a good year for potatoes, although at the end of lifting potatoes we had a lot of rain which made it difficult to get the last few acres out, but the

Page Thirty Two

I get the key of the door

Pollys Farm, this picture was taken over 100 years ago.

potatoes sold well. I remember father telling me that the Red King variety had made £250.00 an acre, that being 10 tons of 'ware potatoes' at £25.00 per ton. He said it was the most money he ever made per acre at farming in his life. As we go on and I am referring to potatoes, in the winter of 1957-58, we sold over £9000.00, worth of potatoes. These were sold to West, the wholesaler at Southend. Because we had made this amount of money, father had the chance to purchase Pollys Farm, from the Smiths. Eventually we bought the farm, after a lot of 'if'ing and butting.'

The next three years were disastrous, '58 was very wet; most of the potatoes went rotten in the ground; what we did get out were only cattle food. '59 was so hot and dry. When we lifted the potatoes, they were like sponges, useless for human consumption, and again became animal food. Then 1960 was another very wet year. The potatoes we managed to get out went rotten in the clamps. In those three years, we only sold £800.00 worth.

This, as you can imagine. put the old overdraft sky high, and that was a very worrying time for all. As I have told you about the potato disaster, I should tell you about the corn harvest. This was nearly as bad as the potatoes. We were having very catchy weather these three years, it did not seem to stop raining. The wheat, oats and barley were stacked damp, with the hope it would dry out before it was threshed, but it did not happen. The merchants would not buy until it was dried down to 16% moisture and the cost was a few £'s per ton, as father exclaimed:

" It takes the icing off the cake!"

Disastrous Fire at Walfords

I got married in May 1960, to the foreman's daughter at Chichester Hall. We lived for a time in a new bungalow on the Hullbridge Road, but things did not work out very well, owing to health reasons. We later divorced, the end of another era. So back to the farms, at least they went on.

Sometime about July 1960, we decided to put in our own corn drier and corn dresser. We bought a 'Ransomes two ton per hour continuous drier and Boby dressing machine.' The next step was to install it, the shed or barn had got to be fairly large, so as to be able to handle the grain we produced. We looked round all the farms and decided the only one that fitted the purpose was the big old Essex Barn at Chichester Hall. The barn still had young cattle in part of it; the other part had all the mixing facilities for the cattle.

We had to build another shed to use as a mixing place for the cattle food. This was built with large wooden sections from disused army huts a lot of these camps were being dismantled now the war was over. Fred Ives, the local second hand timber merchant, bought a considerable amount of these camps, as new timber was still hard to come by; we bought a number of these sections from Fred. I had been a friend of Fred's ever since he came from Dagenham to Shotgate and continued to be a friend, until he passed away.

Norman Ives, Fred's Son, used to come to the Farm on a Saturday afternoon, bring me a bit of wood and have a couple of trusses of hay for his horse. I am pleased to say that Norman is also my friend.

This shed had to be put up in double quick time, the cattle out of the barn, muck cleared out, brick rubble brought in for the base and then concreted over. Most of the time it was Les and myself that did the work connected with installing the machinery. We built two concrete block walls eight feet high, six feet long and four feet apart, We made a platform on top of the walls with 8x3 inch planks. The platform was 12 feet square. We then got the dresser on top and bolted down. As time was running out to get the drier working, we had no time left to put in an elevator and had to make do with a twenty one foot auger. The corn was augured from the floor to the top of the dresser, shaken over the sieves and fell by gravity into the drier which was continuous. When the corn was dried down to 16% you then took the corn off in sacks, mostly weighing two and quarter cwts each at that time.

When I look back to the times when we carried all these heavy sacks, I say to myself:
"No wonder my hips wore out, but when you are young and strong, you never think anything can stop you The man who worked with me to install the machinery was, Les Staines; he used to work for the threshing and combine contractor, named, 'Joe Keeling,' Crays Hill Billericay. When Joe was between seasons, and work was slack, Les came and worked for us; after a couple of seasons he said he would like to stay with us full time. This suited us fine. He could use a combine, baler, plough, crop spraying and could maintain most of the machinery he used. A good all round man, as a team we always got on well together.

Myself (left) with my friend Fred Ives.

[1] A spiral within a tube which when rotated lifts corn etc up the tube to come out at the top.

Disastrous Fire at Walfords

The first year we had the drier, Les dried just over 900 tons of grain. This was not all of our produce; we contracted to dry for a number of merchants, Cramphorns, Matthews, Pertwee, Gould and others. In fact the extra drying we did nearly paid for the original outlay in the first year. When we had a ten ton load ready, we had to get them to collect it quickly to give us the room to receive more in, as we were short of space, although Les stacked the two and quarter cwt sacks three high. When you do that its hard going. In about 1960

rings' with sisal craft paper inside, a bit crude but they did the job and saved a lot of carrying of heavy sacks.

It was about the same time that potatoes were difficult to sell and make a profit, so we decided to try and sell directly to the public. We had a notice board painted "Potatoes for Sale," and we had a retail licence to sell farm produce, so we were not breaking the law. This venture went very slowly at first, then people began to notice the sign and I think we

Ransomes Combine.

we bought our first combine harvester, a 'Ransomes 901 12 foot cut tanker.' The tank held about twenty two cwts when full; this would be augured into 'three ton tipping trailers' and taken to the drier if it needed drying, if not it was put ready to be sold. The following year we put in a 'receiving grainpit' and elevator. This made the job much easier. Also we built a large shed on the back of the barn, again with large wooden sections from Fred Ives. We had started to use bins to put the dried corn into. These bins were 'weld mesh

were one of the first farms to do this sort of trade. When the customers came in for potatoes they would ask for eggs; as we had a few chickens, we began to sell our eggs too.

As trade got better we had to find someone to supply us with good eggs. We got in touch with some friends of ours, Joe and Mary Flemming, Lower Road Hockley. They agreed to supply us. I think I would be right in saying that we sold between 350 and 550 dozen eggs each week, as well as over three and half

Disastrous Fire at Walfords

tons of potatoes. We had built up a good business, but I will say, we did not have a minute to ourselves. We were on the go seven days a week.

In the middle '60's we reduced our milking herd to about 20 cows, really because our way of milking was, by this time, old-fashioned. The milking parlour and covered yard was the thing to do. But as we did not own Walfords Farm, and at this time could not buy it as it was in trust. My father said he could not see his way clear to spend money on other people's property, especially when no help was forthcoming from the trust. So that was the reason why we were cutting out the cows.

In about 1967, my mother was taken ill with excessive nose-bleeds, but I think it saved her from either a brain haemorrhage or heart attack. She had to be very careful as her blood-pressure was always high; none the less, she kept going. After we sold some of the cows we had a spare shed or two and at that time, oats and barley were selling for about £16.00 a ton. I had noticed there were a few riding horses around and young girls were getting their parents to buy them a pony. I had some thoughts in my head about what I would like to try and had a long discussion with father, explaining that if we crushed the oats and put them into half cwt paper bags. We could sell them to the horse owners for round about 30 shillings a cwt, this being a lot better than 16 shillings a cwt.

Although father was not very enthusiastic about it, he said: "Give it a try. "

So the next thing to do was to get my Uncle Tom to get his man to crush the oats, as the crushing machine was at Cracknells Farm, and then bring the crushed oats to Walfords. I had another sign board painted:
"Horse Feed For Sale."

And put it up on one of the sheds. Again, at the start of this project trade was very slow; perhaps I was expecting too much. Anyway, I had some leaflets printed and went to see a few newsagents whom I knew and asked if they had any customers who had horse magazines delivered to them. They said yes, so I then asked them to put my leaflets in the magazines. As word got round, trade got better. But as more customers came in I soon realised they wanted a lot more commodities other than crushed oats, so we crushed barley. Then I went a little further, and bought in a mixed load of broad brans, flaked maize, linseed cake, middling's, pony cubes and a few other things.

As trade grew I had all sorts of people in who kept animals. Once you start these things, and if you are lucky, as we were, then they escalate. You have no idea of how many people keep animals of all kinds. I was asked for rabbit pellets, guinea pig food, well you name it, it was asked for. Now we had reduced our cow herd we had some hay and straw to spare and this was sold to the horse customers. We were now getting a lot of customers coming in, so someone had to be there most of the time. At that time it was not very professional and there was not a lot of room in the old cowsheds to hold stocks. In 1969 we discussed building a new barn.

Well, I had been fairly handy with my hands throughout my short life, so I persuaded father and his brother that I could build a barn. I started this with help from a couple of men off the farm. This work was done in between other farm work. I managed to acquire 15 RSJ's 17 feet long from Fred Ives, and 5 roof trusses with a span of 45 feet, all second-hand, from David Stacey. The idea was to make a barn 60 ft long and 45 ft wide, with a lean-to on one side 60 ft long and 30 ft wide. My old friend Fred Ives came to my aid once again and supplied me with the timber purlings. This was new timber as Fred was now selling new as well as secondhand. We got the holes dug out and the RSJ's concreted in. Now to get the trusses up, we also got the purlings drilled and close by, then I hired a crane and made a start. Standing on the ground and looking at the job, I said to myself :

"Piece of cake with a crane," but I had a rude awakening!

[2] *Rolled steel joists.*

Disastrous Fire at Walfords

When I was up a ladder 14 ft high, with bolts and spanner and the roof truss swinging on the crane, another man with a rope tied to the truss, trying to guide it to me on top of the post to be bolted, that was when I changed my mind about it being a 'piece of cake.' After a lot of hassle we got all the framework assembled, but it was a long hard day. I saw at the start a couple of hours' work to get the job done. How wrong I was!

We eventually got the barn finished, just in time to put the hay into it. It held in the region of twelve to fourteen thousand bales when full. We had finished haymaking, started the corn harvest and filled the remaining part of the barn with straw bales. We also filled the other sheds with straw.

Remains of a Dutch barn at Walfords Farm, Hullbridge, after fire raged through buildings for more than 24 hours.

The burned-out Minivan lies amid the charred ruins of Walfords Farm Hullbridge.

Firemen in farm blaze oil drama

WITH ONLY a trickle of water, firemen today battled to stop a blaze sweeping a farm at Hullbridge. A mini-van exploded, six buildings were destroyed and a tank containing more than 170 gallons of diesel oil threatened to blow up.

And there was not enough pressure from a tiny three-inch water main on the farm for them to use powerful hose jets.

An SOS was sent out for South Essex Water Board to lay on more pressure as farm-workers and firemen dashed to drag three more vehicles clear.

A shower of red-hot corrugated-iron sheets crashed from one building down around firemen.

Four fire engines were trying to draw water from the main and a water expert said the pressure they got would have been similar to a strong kitchen tap flow through each jet using the main.

Full pressure was raised within minutes of a water board inspector arriving at the farm, called Walfords Farm, in Hullbridge Road.

Flames

Two-thirds of the farm's harvest was destroyed.

Mr. John Thorpe, one of two brothers running the farm with their father, said: "That is a year's work gone. About 360 tons of hay and 20 tons of straw have been destroyed."

As well as the mini-van which exploded and burned out, a bale elevator and a chaff cutter were wrecked along with animal feeding sheds, he said.

But the blaze was prevented from reaching the family farmhouse. Wind blew the flames away from it.

Farm workers Bill Searles and Michael Lawrence dashed into one building to rescue three calves only minutes before it collapsed in flames.

NO WATER FOR FARM INFERNO

Reporter: John Ellegard

FIREMEN were helpless

Page Thirty Seven

Disastrous Fire at Walfords

As you might have guessed, we were well into the harvest, nearly finished in fact, when disaster struck. One of the small sheds caught fire and there was a very strong wind. It was not long before the whole lot was ablaze. Two of our men got the five calves out of the shed and saved them. (It was 1st September 1970) The fire service was called and they came very quickly, but the problem was water. They soon sucked the main water dry, as there was no pressure. They had to put three pumps in line, to pump water from Mr Pinkerton's reservoir (a nearby farmer) By this time it was too late to save anything apart from the cowsheds. The new barn went with all the rest of the buildings. The fire was so great that it burnt for seven days. Our family was absolutely devastated. The fire service ran an investigation into how the fire started and came to the conclusion that it was an electrical fault in one of the small sheds.

There were a lot of things to sort out with the insurance companies. We appointed Mr Tony Tanton, of Offin & Rumsey, Rochford, to work for us and he did a very good job. Mr Tanton had to work for the landlord as well as us, as the sheds and barns belonged to the landlord but the new big barn was ours. He worked out that the equivalent size for the landlord was 60ft by 35ft by 13ft to the eves and ours was, as built, 60ft by 45ft by 15ft to the eves, with a 60ft x 30ft leanto. These were agreed, it was also agreed where the new sheds were going to be placed. It was decided to erect the landlord's barn near enough on the old site, and it was to be a universal barn, a bulk grainstore, cattle shed or potato store, having double sliding doors on one side and a single door one end. The other barn would go alongside, leaving a space of 20 feet in between.

Mr Tanton had to get a few quotes from barn builders, and decided on a firm from the North.

But before anything could start, we had to clear the debris of the fire. As luck would have it, we had an old 'International Drott' and this worked well to clear the site. The hardest job was to get all the twisted girders and roof trusses cut up and cleared away, I think it was cleared in about ten days. Building was eventually started and was going well considering it was winter, they had nearly completed, when we had another great shock.

Page Thirty Eight

Sadness and Burdens

On 16th February 1971, my father had a severe coronary and passed away. This was the worst thing that had happened to me in my life so far, because my father and I got on very well and when this happens it hurts so much more. My father had a saying which was:

"You can't stop because of death, you must keep on going, otherwise the world would stop."

So as much as I grieved him passing, this saying I remembered.

When my father died I was 42 years old. I have always told people and friends that I never grew up until that day. They laugh, but I will try to explain what I felt. My father's comments were that I was strong and healthy. I could do the work and look after the farms, and that he could look after all the business side of things. I must say that this suited me, as I did not like doing paper work. I had never seen a bank manager, or even opened a letter to do with the business at all, until the day father died. When father was taken ill the doctor came immediately, but it was so severe, he could not save him, and it was not for the want of trying. It was Doctor

This group from left: Sid Cripps, David Stacey, myself and Sam Stacey.

Glandon Thomas. As well as being our doctor, he was a very good friend. He and his wife stayed with my mother, whilst I went to see my uncle, father's partner, to break the sad news to him. I must say that it 'knocked him for six,' as he had always looked to father as the 'Governor,' so to speak.

The next thing I had to do was to meet the bank manager. This was a job I was not looking forward to, but it had to be done. In a bag there was £1,300.00 that should have been paid in that Tuesday morning, but owing to the circumstances, this had been forgotten. For as long as I can remember, the family had banked on Tuesdays and Fridays, Friday's also to draw their wages. Well, I went to Rayleigh to meet the bank manager for the first time, (the first of many visits). It was a Mr Harry Graham. He invited me into his office and soon put me at my ease. He told me that it was very helpful that the £1,300 had not been banked that morning, as he would have to close the account on my father's death. He also said that my uncle and I would now be partners in, 'T G & J W G Thorpe,' and the £1,300 would start the new account. He then went on to ask who was going to carry on the business side of the farming. He said that if my uncle was going to do it, then he would have to meet him to discuss things with him. But if my uncle wanted me to take on the job, he would then have to sign a document giving me the

My mother and father.

Sadness and Burdens

authority to run the business as father had done previously.

When I went back to uncle and explained the situation to him, he signed the papers gladly. I could see he did not want the responsibility. The next stile to get over was the funeral. There was a large attendance at the funeral, as father was well known in the farming world and over the years he had made a lot of friends and was respected by all. Well, things went along fairly well.

Uncle wanted to see me at least three times a week to have a chat about the farms, and what we were going to do. As it happened, we got on better than we ever had, but saying that, we had always got on well together.

After my father's death we lost the lease on the Ministry of Agriculture's land and had to pay for dilapidations amounting to £1000. 00, this being due to overgrown hedges and ditches. The Land Commission, the name it was now known by, would only have one name on the lease and that was 'A J Thorpe.' After we vacated the land, the head man of the Land Commission came to see me to ask if I would take it on again. I had a discussion with uncle and we decided against it. Uncle said we did not want the trouble of this heavy old land and I agreed. By this time the new barns had been built, so we moved the animal food into the front half of the grain store and clamped potatoes in the back half. In addition, trade was increasing in the animal food business and I considered it to be a good time to increase the variety of products we had to offer.

I bought a mixed lot of chicken feed, layers mash and pellets, growers mash and pellets, rabbit pellets, we created our own mixed corn, (this sold well). I then worked out a mix for horses: this was mixed on the floor with shovels. Then I made a rabbit mix. This consisted of rabbit pellets, flaked maize, crushed oats and crushed barley, again mixed on the floor. The horse mix and rabbit mix sold very well along with pony cubes, hay and straw. As it happened, things were going quite well, I was very pleased and so was uncle, but as we know, all is never plain sailing. On or about the 9th June 1971, uncle was taken ill and on the 16th June he passed away, in very much the same way as father.

This was exactly four months to the day, after father's death. Now I had the same things to do as before. The only difference being that I was left partner with my aunt Lil (uncle's wife). She had to sign the papers this time for me to continue, and again she was pleased to do so. I was not so lucky this time with money. I had written cheques to the value of about £2000.00 the day before uncle had died and posted them, but the bank would not let this money come out of that account. So I had to start another account in the names of J W G Thorpe and L G Thorpe, so trading. Also on a £2000.00 overdraft, but as they say, that's life!

As you can imagine, the next milestone was, DEATH DUTIES. I put all the legal business of the two brothers into the hands of our solicitors, 'F D Todman and Sons of Rayleigh,' who had dealt with the families legal problems for many years. As you can

Father's brother, my Uncle Tom at milking time.

Sadness and Burdens

imagine, these things take a long time to sort out, and so time went by. I used to pay my aunt a wage from the business, the same as I would take. She also had a box of greengrocery each week, as by this time we were selling produce at the door, so it was easy to give aunt a box.. As time went on, I think my cousin had an argument with his mother, and aunt went to live with her relations in Haverhill, Suffolk. I would then send her a weekly cheque until she finally returned.

would mean both of us and she agreed. I forgot to mention that I had bought a bungalow some years before this and had to sell it, but I'd made a substantial profit, and could have paid my share of the death duties. But I had lent some of the money to the partnership to buy a new combine. This was agreed between uncle and myself before he died. It was 'all above board' and uncle agreed. This is the reason I said if my aunt wanted her share of the duties to come from the business, then so should mine. To coin

Myself ploughing.

It was about this time that the solicitors requested me to go and see them. They told me that 'crunch time had come' (or words to that effect) and that the district valuer had come to a decision as to the amount of death duties on the brothers. They also told me they had tried time and again to get a reply from either my aunt or my cousin, but to no avail.

They also explained that it was up to the beneficiaries to pay the duties. I said I would contact my aunt and try to get some sort of answer. I had a discussion with aunt and cousin, aunt said she had no money to pay the duty and asked what she should do. I told her the only thing I could suggest was to pay it from the farming business. This I said

a phrase, 'what's good for the goose is good for the gander'. It was now back to the solicitors. I told them they would have to deal with me for both of the duties. They told me it was nearly £16,000.00. By this time, what with one thing and another, I was getting "*#*** off ' (fed up) and told the solicitors to offer the district valuer £200.00 per month until it was paid up. This they said they would do, but did not think he would accept. Then in temper I said,

"Then tell him to sell us up."

Anyway it did not come to that: he accepted our offer and we paid on the 11th of each month. The solicitors account was £1000.00, but they were very helpful and let me pay in two installments.

Page Forty One

Sadness and Burdens

When the bank learned of the deal I had struck with the district valuer, they offered to loan me the money to pay it off, but I declined the offer, as the bank wanted 18% interest and the district valuer wanted 3%: a big difference.

What I have not said is when uncle died we got notice to quit Chichester Hall Farm. Now that both brothers had died I had no hold on the lease, so out we had to come. They 'dilapidated us' £2000.00 on the farm, but this was off-set against the buildings we had erected for the drying sheds and cattle yards. The drying and cleaning machinery was moved to Cracknells Farm. This was installed in a 60 x 40 foot concrete barn.

Well, things went along steadily, we had 'got out of cows' completely by now, and also all the dry stock, so all our grass land had to be cut and baled. This was no worry as we had a good trade in hay and straw, through the feed business and were selling in the region of 20,000 bales a year. It was still seven days a week for us, as my cousin did not want to work at week-ends. I used to do all sorts of jobs on the farm, as well as some deliveries of hay, straw and hard feed. By this time we had a three ton box van. It had to be a covered lorry to keep the feed dry, as it was all packed in paper bags. In the winter we were very busy on the animal feed side. It worked out quite well really, because when the weather got better, round about May – June, trade dropped off, giving us more time for hay making and the harvest.

It was about this time that I met a lady friend, Lilian Laver, who was living in Rayleigh. She had some marital problems and was looking for work. Lilian had been doing homework for 'M K Electric,' but it was rather boring. As I have said I did a lot of different jobs and Lilian came down to the farm to help in the shop and the feed store. While I was ploughing at Rawreth during weekends, or whenever, she would look after the feed store on her own. This was more than helpful, as it allowed me to do a lot more work on the farm. An arrangement which suited us both, especially as Lilian was familiar with farm work having been a 'land girl' in 'WW2.'

However, as time went on, I was having trouble agreeing with my cousin, I don't know when it started, but there came a time when I just could not do anything right for him, no matter how much I tried, but I didn't really fall out with him. I must say though, I was getting sick and tired of his moans and groans. One day I was feeling 'very down' after listening to him going on about all and sundry. Anyway after he had gone, I went to the house where mother and Lilian were having a cup of tea, They both asked what was the matter, I told them and went on to say that I had had enough and that I had a 'good mind' to hand in my notice. Lilian looked at me and said:

"How can you hand in your notice, when you are the 'guvn'r'?"

I explained that I meant, hand in my notice to the partnership. Well! They both stared at me for a while, then Lilian said:

"If you have made up your mind that is what you want to do, then I for one, will stand by you," and mother agreed.

Lilian, in her WW2 uniform of the "Woman's Land Army."

A Fresh Clean Start

With a little push from them both I went to the Solicitors straight away. My notice was sent to my aunt. I must say I felt very sorry, as my aunt had never given me any trouble at all and was always pleased to see me. But it so happened that she was my partner. After my aunt received my notice she was very upset, I do not think my cousin could do anything to calm her. He rang me up and said that I had upset his mother so much, and he wanted me to go and put things right. Lilian, in her wisdom, said I should not go alone, and that I should have a witness. So I rang a mutual friend of my aunt and myself, Joe Flemming, and he came with me.

We met my aunt, cousin and his wife. They tried very hard to get me to alter my decision, but I stuck to my guns. I told them all that Alan was not happy about how I was running the farming business, so I was giving him the chance to do his own thing and then he had only got himself or his mother to answer to. Any money he made would be his and his mother's, to do with as they pleased. I also told him to get his valuers to sort the split out and he could do it any way he liked. I would not stand in his way at all. Anyway, they kept Cracknells Farm, house and buildings, approximately 85 acres, also two 'Ford 4000' tractors, ploughs, disc harrows, mower, combine, drier and corn augers, tipping trailers, four wheel trailers and an oat crusher. I was left with 60 acres at Pollys farm 40 acres at Rawreth, plus a bungalow in which an employee lived. He worked for me. There were two old 'Fordson Majors,' disc's, plough, old baler and bits and pieces of 'one thing and another'.

I rented Walfords. The land that my father had vested in our joint names, John and Alan Thorpe and had only cost £1,300.00. Alan did not want his half share. I told him to get it valued and I would buy it. This cost me £9,500.00 The only good thing about it was that I now had some land worth more than £19,000.00. I then owned 134 acres. As for Walfords, there are people about who will do you a big favour without any financial reward. Mr Donald Tanton of Rochford was this kind of gentleman. After my uncle died he granted a lease in my sole name, so when I parted company from the partnership, Alan said to me:

"You have only got another year on the lease at Walfords, and then you will have to get out."

Well, when I told him of the lease in my own name, he got rather upset.

As far as the animal feed business went, we had run the stocks down to practically nil; the hay and straw was valued and I paid my half share. The corn stocks at Cracknells was sold and the proceeds shared. Alan had a letter sent to me stating that I could not trade under the name of G A Thorpe & Sons. This did not bother me in the least, Lilian said:

"Why not trade under your own name? Everybody knows John Thorpe."

So this we did. The week before we ended the partnership, I had a friend with a '40ft artic trailer,' and he picked up 20 tons of mixed animal food for me. We parked it at Dollimans Farm, by kind permission of Mr Peter Philpot.

My cousin and me parted company on the Saturday and closed everything up and on Sunday we brought in the load of feed and were ready to open on Monday morning, trading as 'John Thorpe Forage Merchants and Farmers.' One thing I did find after we had split up was that I had a lot of very good friends. The first year on my own was very tight, with very little money, but we managed. We got all the land planted with wheat, barley, and oats. And looked forward to better times ahead.

When hay time came round we had a baler, not a very good one, but a baler! Anyway, we got through hay baling, carted and stacked it in the barn. Now the harvest was a different matter!. I had been dealing with a Mr Biff Rayner of Churchend Farm, Paglesham. I was out of crushed oats one Saturday morning and I rang him to see if he had any to sell. He had and was good enough to let me go and collect some. That saw us over the weekend as we did most trade on a

A Fresh Clean Start

Saturday or Sunday. This was the first time I had had any dealings with Mr Rayner, although my father had done a few deals with his father. He was the gentleman who got us into Walfords in 1942. By contacting Biff that Saturday we had a good business arrangement for a few years, with crushed oats, barley, hay and straw. Mr Rayner was always very helpful to me. When we were talking about harvest one day, he said he would try to combine my corn for me, but due to the weather he got behind and could not do it. He said he would take my wheat and oats and store them for me, and he would leave a 20 ton bulk trailer in the field for me to fill.

I borrowed an old 'Ransomes Cavalier Combine,' it was not very good, but we made a start and got through a lot of the wheat. But I had 20 acres of oats at Rawreth that were as 'flat as a pancake' and the combine could not take it. The pick up cog had stripped its teeth and we could not get a new one.

I was in a bit of a quandary to know what to do; then I thought of Mr Sam Stacey. I had had some deals with him and his brother David, with beet pulp when we fed it to our stock. They used to grow sugar beet and after the sugar has been extracted then a percentage

Sam Stacey's combine.

is given back as pulp. I had heard that he had finished the harvest, so I rang him to see if he could come and combine the oats for me. He told me his combine was at his brother Peter's farm at Hanningfield. With no hesitation, he said if he came over and I went with him to escort him back, then he would help me. Well, we got the combine to the field: his was a 'New Holland Combine' and in comparison to the 'Ransomes,' it was a 'Rolls Royce.' Anyway, we started off and Sam was showing me all the workings of the combine. At the time I wondered why. I was soon to find out. After we had been up and down the field twice, he said:

"Right, do you think you can handle it now ? I have got an appointment."

My only answer was:

"I hope so !"

I kept going steadily and I can tell you it was a pleasure after the old Ransomes Combine. I then thought, as it was going so well, I could go a little faster. That was my undoing! By going faster I blocked the drum. After about half an hour's *#*#*#* hard work, I got it unblocked, and got going again.

I had learnt my lesson, (go steady). Looking back to that time, Sam did me a great favour. How many other people would have let me have a combine and leave it with me to cut my corn? I cannot think of anyone. Also, he did not charge me a penny for it: That is good friendship.

Biff Raynor, relaxing at his farm . Church End, Paglesham.

Lows and Highs

It was about this time that I became friendly with a man who was in the haulage business, working for Fords at Basildon. He asked me if he could store some tractor tyres on the farm. I was told that they were all straight and above board and that there was no problem with them. He added that by working for the Ford Company he could get them very cheaply and that I could sell them to farmer friends of mine and he would 'give me a drink'. As I learned later, I was very naïve, I believed all I was told. He was also able to obtain 'paper work' for items Fords had to sell, 'paper work' which they normally used internally and related to surplus items. Such as lorries, vans, tractors, trailers, engines in fact anything they had finished with. Fords kept all of these at a place called 'Frog Island,' potential buyers could then get a pass to go and look at what was available and if you were interested in anything you then put your price against the item and handed your bid in. You were informed later if your bid was accepted.

I had sold some of these tyres to a man who repaired tractors. He rang me one evening and asked if the man who sold the tyres could get engines, I said I would ask him, or if he liked he could ring and speak to him himself. He said he would rather I did it for him, so this I did. About three weeks later I had a phone call to say that four engines were available and the price was £800.00: would I see if the man wanted them? This I did and he said he would have them, providing they were good engines.

Some time later the engines were delivered to the customer, and he told the person who delivered them he had not got enough cash to pay for them. As I heard later the delivery man said:

"That's all right, make the cheque out to John Thorpe, he will cash it for us."

This is what I did and I paid the cheque in the bank with all our other takings. About three weeks later, the haulage man turned up on a Saturday morning with two lorries. I asked what he wanted. He went on to tell me then that the police had been to the man who had bought the engines and they would be coming to me, as the engines had been stolen. Because the cheque had been made out to me, clearly I was the one who had sold them to him. I asked him about the tyres and he said he had got to shift them quickly before the police came, as they were not 'kosher'. It then struck me they were stolen as well. He shifted all the tyres out and was gone.

On the Monday morning a lot of police came and turned the place over. There was nothing on the farm that shouldn't be, but as they had the cheque written out to me they were adamant that I had sold the engines. As the police could not find the real culprit I was the one who had to take the brunt of the case. Two days before I went to court, two men came into the yard and asked if I was John Thorpe. I nodded and they said:

"Don't go in the witness box when you get to court, otherwise either the farm goes up, or your wife".

With that they were gone.

Of course I didn't go in the box and I was sentenced to twelve months in prison. My barrister did appeal but at the appeal the three Judges openly said they now knew the man who committed the crime, and named him. However, because I would not go into the witness box and name the man I would have to serve the sentence I was given, owing to the great amount of money involved. I'm not just saying it to try and cover myself. Lilian and a good friend of ours were in court and can bear out what the Judges had to say. Anyway, I only served eight months after a remission of four months for good behaviour. All of my friends did what they could to help while I was away, especially Jim Parker, Sam Stacey and many others. Thank you all!

In about 1977-78 we had a very wet winter and my land at Pollys Farm was in a sorry state. It was literally flooded. Sam and another friend of mine, Mr Sid Cripps, a mushroom grower and farmer of Pond Chase Nurseries, were looking at the boggy state of the fields, and Sam said:

Page Forty Five

Lows and Highs

"You are never going to grow anything on this land until it is drained."

This meant going to the bank and trying for a loan. The bank manager then was Mr Peter Keith, another very helpful man. He arranged a loan for the drainage. Sam looked after the job from start to finish. He had quite a lot of knowledge about drainage. He had the water diverted right round the perimeter of the farm, hedges and ditches grubbed out and all tile pipes laid by 'Pearl Land Drainage.' When all the tiles were laid, Sam mole-ploughed it himself. When the moleing was finished, Sam loaned me a tractor and plough, so that two tractors would get the job done quicker.

The retail animal food store and the two lorries I purchased from Fred Ives.

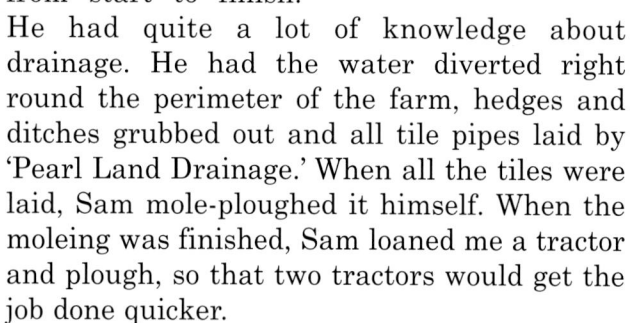

Both ploughs were reversibles, these ploughs enabled the land to be kept on the flat once it was drained. When it was all cleared and ploughed it looked a vast area. I had a lot of help from all my friends. When Sid had any spare time from his mushroom farm he would come along and help, with his son Tim. While we are talking about Sid, I will tell you a little of what I know about him. He started his working life as a blacksmith's mate, or, as they used to call them, a 'striker'. I don't know how long he did this job, but whatever he learnt stood him in good stead all his life. I think he then worked for a Mr Stacey at Southminster, Sam and David's father. By this time, Sid was getting keen to be his own master and he told me he had bought a piece of land in Southminster and for a year or two, grew a lot of vegetables and different seeds for seed salesmen. Eventually, Sid decided to take Pond Chase Nurseries, Hockley. He started with next to nothing, but by sheer hard work and grit was very, very successful. I don't think any man has worked harder. One thing I must say:

"I am lucky to have him as a friend."

After all the land was ploughed, Sam said we should put it all into winter wheat, so we rolled, disked and springtined the field which produced a fair seed bed; then I drilled the wheat. When it grew, it looked as if I had missed a row every drill width. Sam and Sid 'took the rise' out of me, and said I should buy another drill with an extra row on it. I knew as soon as I saw it, what I had done wrong, I had driven the tractor wide of the marker.

When we came on to winter, the animal feed side came into its own. We were increasing our trade all the time. It was becoming a full time job for two men and a boy in the store, as well as Lilian being full time in the office, writing out orders for deliveries, and answering the phone. Orders used to come in up to ten o'clock at night. As I said, a full time job.

My friend Fred Ives, the timber merchant, came over to see me one day. He told me he was changing his lorries and asked me if I would like to buy one of the old ones. I said I would like to have one, knowing he had always kept them in good condition. I thought this would be useful, to collect some of the feed we sold, so I bought it from him, but when I say bought, I mean he nearly gave it to me. (Another good friend). We found a lot of work for this lorry. When bran was very short, Mr Pat Rankin made arrangements for me to collect five tons from 'Whitworths of Northampton'. The lorry went

Page Forty Six

Lows and Highs

well. Also, I used to go to 'Edwards Mill' at Bishops Stortford to collect broad bran as we had a good demand for all these type of feeds. This was arranged by Pat Rankin, I got on very well with Pat and he helped me in my feed business in many ways.

At a later date, Fred offered me another of his lorries. I had that one as well and it carried six tons. We used to go every Tuesday to collect flake maize, flake barley, chicken pellets, rabbit pellets and other feed from 'Hitchcocks Mills' at Fingringhoe, near Colchester. The lorry was a good old servant, until the stupid driver I employed at that time drove it without a fanbelt, and boiled it dry. As you can guess he 'killed it.' After that, we had got so used to collecting our own feed that we had to find another lorry.

We bought a ten ton Leyland from 'Hitchcocks' at Fingringhoe, where we collected our feed from and ran that for a few years. We also had at this time two box vans, one seven and the other a three ton 'Ford Cargo'. The first lorry I had from Fred was still going strong.

Another good friend of ours was Jim Parker, who worked for the Philpot family, as an accountant. Jim and his

My friend of many years, Jim Parker.

wife Rene had a potato business, delivering potatoes to shops - especially fish shops. They used to go out twice a week, Tuesdays and Thursdays. They also collected their potatoes from farms and stored them at Walfords. This worked very well. Jim, being an accountant, helped me considerably with my paper work, I could not have done without him. He was always there to help when we had business problems and when we had health troubles.

When Sid Cripps wasn't tending his mushrooms or helping me on my farm he was flying his aeroplane around Europe.

Page Forty Seven

Lows and Highs

Building our first grain store for 300 tons of grain. Ernie Barton was a great help to me in the building of this store. Also a very good tractor driver, Ernie could turn his hand to most jobs on the farm.

After a few years the lorry was getting past its best. Jim and Rene bought their own lorry, parked it at Walfords and still ran their potato business. I had not been away on holiday until I was 43 years old, then I went to Majorca with some friends; the next holiday was at Tenerife. Now, since meeting Jim and Rene, the four of us have travelled widely in England, have gone eight times to Portugal and three times to Tenerife. I think we have made up for lost time.

Now we were producing a lot more grain, due to land drainage and the ploughing up of more grassland. We needed a grain store, so we required another bank loan to build a barn 80 ft by 50ft, open sided.

The barn was completed and the first year we filled it with hay and straw. When we had cleared half of the barn, we started to make the grain store. We used 'Bentalls grain walling.' This was specially formed sheets of galvanised iron that was bolted to RSJs, spaced seven feet apart. After we had erected the walling, we then had to concrete the floor, leaving channels three feet apart, eighteen inches deep. These channels had gratings on the top, to let air through. These were named 'choc-blocs.' You had a large main tunnel on the end of the barn, with a large fan to blow dry air through the grain to dry it. The store, after it was completed, held 300 tons of corn.

Two tractors at work planting wheat on Walford farm.

Lows and Highs

Two years later we added another bay to hold a further 300 tons. This bay did not have any drying facilities, but none the more for that it was a good store. Now we had made this barn into a grain store, we were short of storage for hay and straw. We had another barn built, 80ft by 80ft. This held a lot of hay and straw. We used to have over 40 thousand bales of hay and a few thousand of straw per year. This was all sold through the feed side of the farming. At the peak of our animal feed business, our turnover was in excess of £400,000, per year, that was without our corn and rape production. We had ploughed up all of our remaining grassland so the farm was now all arable. About 240 acres, rotating four wheats and one oil seed rape. Sam would grow the rape on our land, as he was still doing our combining and was geared up for the rape job. Sam also used to contract rape cutting for a lot of other farmers. I helped him whatever way I could; at times this was a day and night job.

By us being all arable now, we had to buy standing crops of grass on other farms amounting to some 140 acres. We would top dress this with two cwts of nitrogen per acre, to get a good yield. We used to travel as far as West Horndon, to make hay, about 18 miles each way. It was an 80 acre field, with an air strip through the middle; that left us with about 65 acres for hay. Between David Stacey, John Robinson and myself, we had a lot of trailers. I had two 40 ft 'arctic trailers,' and five smaller Scammel trailers. I had made bogies for these to be towed with a tractor. David had one 40 ft and two 35ft 'arctic trailers' and used to loan them to us. David also had a 'Daf Unit' with which to tow the trailers and he used to help us cart the hay home to Walfords. I had made bogies for the large trailers, so we could tow them with the tractors. Sam would come and help us load the hay, so we could get it all on wheels. We have had as many as 5000 bales on trailers at one time. Then there is some work to get them unloaded and stacked in the barns. David also had a 20 ton bulk grain trailer and carted his wheat, and rape to the mills. We had a couple of good lorry drivers, and David would loan us the unit to cart our grain as well. Before this we used tractors and bulk trailers, carrying about 14 tons. I personally had four tractors: these were all Fords a 6600, 6700, two wheel drive, a 7710 and a 'TW 20' four wheel drive. You needed a big tractor to pull a 40ft trailer loaded with 575 bales of hay. If I was ever short of a tractor, Sam, David or Sid, would always loan me one, or even two. As I said, I have got a lot of very good friends, although I have done my best to help them, I am sure I have always been on the winning side.

When the time came round for the lorries to be tested, we all worked together to get them in tip top condition to pass the test. We had a few hic-ups at times, but generally managed to get them through the test. When you have got lorries, tractors and all manner of farm machinery, you have always got to be repairing one thing or another. I used to let a friend of mine use my workshop on the farm, as we had quite a good selection of workshop machinery, pillar drills, power hacksaw, grinding wheels, electric welders, bar-benders and also gas welding and cutting. All through my life, I have had a love for tools of all descriptions and I still have. The friend that used my workshop was Bernard Bleach, he is a very good welder, and fabricator. In fact he built his own truck in the workshop. It took him five years, but that was not full time, he did it when he was slack on other jobs. And it ran very well.

A "Homemade" Car

It all started when I bought two lengths of box iron, 5" by 2½", to make extensions for our fork lift. Well, they were not quite wide enough to slide over the fork lift tines and they lay in the workshop for a few weeks and then Bernard asked if he could have them. I said:

"Yes, what are you going to do with them?"

"I would like to build my self a truck," he replied.

So it was started. The pieces of box iron were cut and formed into the shape of the chassis. The next thing he bought was the front and back axles from a 'Jaguar XJ6,' (bearing in mind that all the parts were good second hand, from local scrap yards in the area) materials he used, the vehicle was a work of art. The motor, or shall we say truck, was built in the style of a 'Jeep' and when it was finished, the job then was to get it on the road. Bernard applied to the Vehicle Registration Office and they sent an inspector to look at it. He passed it and told Bernard to get an MOT certificate. This it also passed. The next job was to get it licensed, so he went to Chelmsford licensing office. They asked him the name of the vehicle: He told them that it had a Leyland engine and a Leyland badge on the front. They told him he could not call it a Leyland, for if he did, he would have a libel court case on his hands. So he said:

"Well it was built on Walfords Farm, can I call it a 'Walford'?"

The Walfords truck.

He then bought a Leyland four cylinder diesel engine. The 'Jag' axles he rebuilt with box iron to make them a lot stronger. The radiator grill was made from a stainless steel drum from an industrial washing machine. All the doors and door hinges, front and rear bumpers, he made from stainless steel channel. From the

So it was named 'Walford,' and the 'Walford' motor is still running about today. Between us over the years, we have made many things. One day I was looking for some flat galvanised iron sheets, I came across the very sheets I needed in Dick Franklin's scrap yard at Benfleet. These were

Page Fifty

A "Homemade" Car

new, but had been marked with water and were going cheap. The size of the sheets were 8ft by 4ft and 8ft by 3ft. As Dick would not split them up, I had to take all that was on the pallets. He put them over the weighbridge and you paid by weight. After I got home and thought about the metal and the cost, I soon realised it was cheap. So I sent one of my lorries and told the driver to bring back the rest of the sheets, saying that there couldn't be more than a couple of tons in weight. How wrong can one be? When Kevin returned and told me that it weighed eight and a half tons, I was rather taken aback, but I remembered my father's words from the past:

"Be a man Jack and stand by what you have said or done!"

Anyway, I did not know what I was going to do with all those sheets, but as I said, we made a lot of things. We started to make doors for our grain stores: these were large sliding doors. The size was 10ft x 15ft and there were two doors to a bay, I think we made about fourteen of these doors and quite a few smaller ones. Some of these were for Sam and David Stacey and some for Sid Cripps. All in all, buying these sheets worked out well in the end.

All of these building and fabricating jobs had to be done when you had time to spare from the farm's demands. When we had finished harvest we would start to plough the land ready for the next year. Farming and growing never stops!

After we had got a few acres ploughed and left it for about two days of drying, we would flat roll it to get it down tight, so it would not dry out too much. It also made it much better with the other cultivations, to get a seed bed. We had to borrow a heavy flat roll for this job; if the roll was not heavy enough, then you could fill it with water to give more weight.

After borrowing Sam's roll for a few years, Bernard and myself got started to make one. We made it on the lines of the one we borrowed from Sam but we decided to make it slightly larger. I went to Bob Ray at South Fambridge and bought a large steel tube, 12ft long 2ft 9ins in diameter. We cut round discs from a sheet of 3/8 steel plate, one for each end and another for the centre, each with a 4in hole through the centre. We then put a heavy tube through and welded it all up: the 3ins axle went through the tube. The frame and drawbar were made with 8"x 3" channel iron, the bearings were made from hard wood, as wood does not wear out like ball bearings do, as long as you gave the wood plenty of grease. When we finally finished the roll, the next thing was to try it. We had a 'Ford 6600 Tractor'; on twin 14-34 rear wheels that we used for rolling. We coupled this to our superb roll to see how it went, but to our dismay the tractor would not get enough

Rape swather.

Page Fifty One

The Ploughing Match

Rochford Hundred Agricultural Society, selection of trophies.

Sam Stacey and Arthur Wallaker in the ploughing match with Brigadier and Noble.

Part of the display of vintage tractors.

Competitor's tractor in front of barn filled with bales of hay.

The stars of the show, Brigadier and Noble.

Lilian presents his trophy to Mr. Fenner who won the vintage ploughing match. Sadly that evening Mr. Fenner died of a heart attack.

Roger Burroughs receiving his trophy.

A vintage caterpillar tractor.

at Walfords Farm 1985

Vintage tractor in the ploughing match.

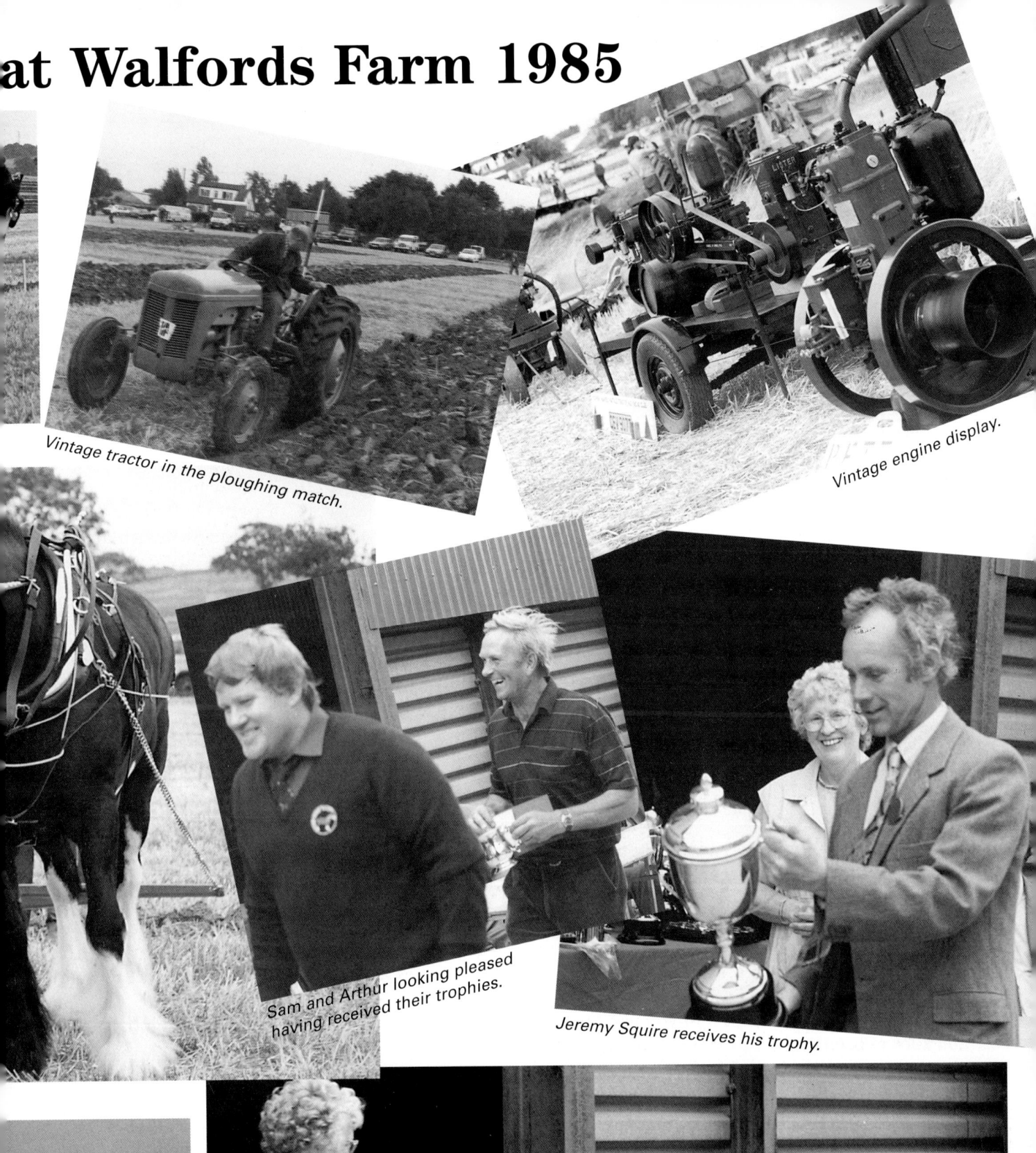

Vintage engine display.

Sam and Arthur looking pleased having received their trophies.

Jeremy Squire receives his trophy.

Lilian presents me with the prize for the best oats.
By tradition the president doesn't enter any of the competitions. However, in this case when it came to the presentation for the best oats, there were no entries. So one of the judges nipped into the barn behind, gathered a bag of oats and entered them on my behalf. I won first prize!

A "Homemade" Car

grip to pull it up hill, so as they say, 'back to the drawing board'. Anyway, Sam came the next day. He had always been interested in the making of the roll; when I told him of our problem, he immediately said:

"I will swap you with my roll,"

to which I simply replied:

"OK."

And this solved our problem.

For a few years now, most of we farmers had been growing oil seed rape and the job was far easier than it was back in the war years. At that time it was hard going; you had to cut it by hand, let it ripen, then cart it to the threshing machine to be threshed. Now they have machines called 'rape swathers'. With these machines you cut the rape and if possible, leave the stubble about 6-9ins high. This then holds the swath off the ground and lets it dry and ripen. Then it is combined. Sam put a lot of hard work and money into the rape crop. At one time he had three 'rape swathers' and contracted to swath some 3000 acres in Essex and other districts, some far away.

They had a two-way radio system to keep in contact with the machines in the event of breakdowns. We had a base at Walford's Farm so as to get a greater coverage, I used to help to move the cutters from farm to farm, sometimes doing a stint at driving and helped to repair the machines when they broke down. If the ground was rough, you would then get a lot of breakages. Later on, I couldn't help as much as I would have liked to have done, as my hips were playing me up, due to arthritis. My doctor sent me to Southend Hospital. They in turn sent me to the Middlesex in London. This went on for a couple of years. By this time I was being pushed by Lilian and friends to 'go private,' but up until this time I had not done so. I must say, when it comes to Hospitals, I am not a very brave man.

In the beginning of 1985, Mr Tony Tanton came to see me, asking me to be President of the 'Rochford Hundred Agriculture Society' for a year, I declined, as I have never liked to be in the public eye, but Lilian and Tony between them persuaded me to take it on. This meant that the annual Ploughing Match would be held on our farm.

This entailed quite a lot of planning. Most of this was carried out by Tony Tanton and Bob Holland plus a little by ourselves. When the time came we had to get the harvest done as soon as possible, so as to get the land cleared, straw baled and stacked in the barns. Sam helped us as well; he came and combined our wheat before he did his own, so we had time to get our other jobs done; in fact everybody joined in to help. Arthur Wallaker, another friend, loaned his caravan with awning to use as the President's tent, so that neighbouring farmers and friends could have a drink with the president. All our wheat we sold and delivered to Allied Mills Rochford. This was to get the barns empty to put the tables and chairs in, as they served a lot of meals on the day of the match.

The week before the match a lot of preparations had to be made, plots to be marked out for the different classes of tractors and ploughs. As well as the normal plough men, there was the vintage class: these were old tractors and ploughs tenderly restored by their owners and entered into competitions. There were also other dedicated enthusiasts who re-store stationary engines, of all makes and sizes, and exhibit at all manner of functions throughout the year. We also had four or five teams of heavy horses ploughing at the match.

Sam and Arthur's hobby is shire horses. They were both there, as they worked together with their horses. All the teams were turned out very smart, but I must say that Sam and Arthur's were exceptional. We were all praying for a nice fine day on that Saturday, in September 1985. When the day came it was a worrying time for me , as all our barns were full to capacity with hay and straw and with a few hundred people roaming about, it was a great fire risk.

And although it was long ago, the disastrous fire at Walfords was still a vivid frightening memory.

Hips, Hay and Harvest

We managed to get all our land planted by the middle of November, this then gave us time to do a lot of other jobs, mostly repairs to tractors, implements and making sure that all the haymaking machinery is all in good working order. It also gave me time to think about having my hip repaired as I had been waiting for a very long time for an appointment at the Middlesex Hospital but I still had no date and Lilian thought I had better get someone else to do it. Well, by about February 1986, I did eventually pluck up the courage to go and see a surgeon, Mr Haywood Waddington of Chelmsford. He said he would do a replacement 'hip job' for me and it was agreed that I would go into the Nuffield Hospital Brentwood on the 7th March 1986. First we had to have x-rays taken at Chelmsford Hospital. After that was done, Lilian was speaking to the radiographer and telling him that I was going to have the bad hip done. He asked which one was that, as he could not see any difference between them. She told him I had been hanging about a couple of years for a bed. Anyway, I had the left hip replaced. A few days after the 'op', a nurse told me they were going to get me on my feet, but there would have to be an x-ray first, to make sure everything was OK. This was done and I quite expected them to let me get up. They didn't come to me for a long time. When they did I asked:

"When are you going to get me up?"

A winter's scene at Walfords.

The doctors kept putting me off and replying, that they had got to wait for Mr Waddington.

At about 5 pm, Mr Waddington appeared and questioned me, as to if I had twisted or turned in the bed. I said I did not think so – why? He then explained that my hip had dislocated and that he would have to operate again, I said:

"Tomorrow ? "

He replied:

"No tonight!"

With that he gave a terrific yawn and said:

"I've been operating at Black Notley Hospital all day and I feel tuckered out."

You can imagine how that made me feel, me not being very brave in hospital at the best of times. Well, eventually I was taken to the operating theatre and the hip was put back into place. They also screwed an extra piece onto the cup to stop it coming out again. A few days later they got me up and walking and eventually told me I could go home. I got on very well for a time, I should say a few months, then I had an abscess come up on my left hip. This caused a great deal of discomfort and pain. I then had to attend Broomfield Hospital. I was then admitted and put on irrigation for two weeks; after which they told me I had got septicaemia. I used to buy the 'East Anglian Times' each day, until I read of a man in Ipswich dying from this complaint. I never bought the paper again. Anyway, after a lot of tablets of all kinds, in fact at one time it was thirty five a day, Lilian had to draw up a graph, so that I would know when and what to take. That was after I was sent home. It was a long old haul to get my blood right.

I was on crutches and in a wheel chair for six months, I had visions of never being able to walk again without the aid of crutches, but eventually they succeeded in getting my blood correct and day by day I became more mobile. After a few months, Mr Waddington then made arrangements for me to go into Broomfield Hospital, and have my other hip replaced.

This time all went well. I was soon out of hospital and home once more. All the time I was off sick and in hospital, Lilian

Hips, Hay and Harvest

had a hard old time, what with looking after the feed business and coming to see me when I was in hospital; it was more than a full time job. After seeing me, she had to get home and write all the delivery tickets out for the next day. At times I know she never got finished until after eleven o'clock at night. A long day for anyone. If anybody deserves a medal, then Lilian does: she has been my greatest asset. After coming out of hospital I got on fairly well, I was able to drive a tractor and do a lot of jobs, but soon found out that I was only a quarter of the man I once was, but nevertheless, I was there to 'shout the odds,' and give the orders. One thing I did miss more than anything else was I could not carry or lift anything heavy, because in our feed business it was all lifting, bales of hay and straw, carrying bags of feed and putting it into motors. This could be quite awkward at times, so I had to keep away from this if I could. But it's the same old thing, when I saw a few customers waiting to be served I would go and try to help, I never liked to keep customers waiting, I like to think we looked after all our customers well and I know the answer was, our thriving business. Our main problem with the hay making was unloading and stacking it in the barns; it was heavy hard and hot work, but it was something that had to be done.

We bought a 'Sanderson Telliporter,' that is a large fork lift four-wheel drive with four-wheel steer. We fitted a grab on the front. This was driven by hydraulics and picked up eight bales at a time. We used this for loading and unloading in the barns. It saved a lot of hand work but it was never as neat and tidy as stacking by hand. But as they say, "that's progress."

We had bought a disused barn from Milton Keynes that had been dismantled by the company which had built my existing barns. I decided I would like to extend our grain store, but I was not to sure how to go about it, mostly because of my inability to climb about and lift heavy iron. Anyway, I had a young man working for me at that time, Kevin Collins. I had taught him most of the things he could do on the farm. So without more ado we got started, Kevin doing most of the work with me planning and as usual 'shouting the odds.' We got on quite well. The holes were dug and filled with concrete with wragg bolts set in, to bolt the stanchions onto. After we had got this all lined up, we hired a crane to lift the roof trusses into place and then bolt all the purlings on. I was pleased with the progress we had made. It all lined up with the adjoining building very well, a few bits were welded here and there and the job was done. Then I went and found some asbestos sheets and Kevin, with my instructions, put the roof on. The following year we made the sliding doors and put in a grain and elevator pit, concreted the floor. We used this new barn to store and to crush oats and barley. This was all sold through the animal feed side of the farm.

Thinking back, we had a very wet harvest, all corn had to be dried. Again Sam having a portable drier, once more came to the rescue and we got through harvest after a struggle, but it did not stop there.

We could not get onto some of the land to plough and not only that, we couldn't bale or burn the straw to get some of the fields clear, but as I have said before, you have to keep trying. We eventually got our seeding finished, but the result wasn't up to our usual standard due to the very poor conditions that autumn and we did wonder about the harvest to come.

The following harvest was indeed a very lean affair. It was only our animal feed business that kept us afloat. The year after that was a great deal better; we got all our haymaking done in good time and all stacked in the barns ready for the winter sales. We always tried to get the hay cleared up and out of the way before the corn harvest. We would then sweep all the grain stores out and fumigate them ready for grain to be tipped in and stored. It was sometime in 1978 that I had a visit from Mr Tony Tanton. We were having a chat about how the farming and the feed business was going. Then he went on to say:

"You know John you can buy Walfords now."

Hips, Hay and Harvest

That unexpected offer startled and surprised me a bit I asked the reason for offering the farm for sale, knowing the farm was in trust to a dog's home. It was at the time when property was at its peak and the trustee's thought if they sold the farm and invested the money they would get a far greater return on the money invested. Certainly considerably more than I was paying in rent. Tony asked if I thought I could raise the money. I told him I would go to the bank and see if they could help. We had spent a lot of money on draining and grubbing out hedges, plus building big barns. At this time, all our spare cash went back into the farming business. Anyway, I made an appointment to see the bank manager, Mr Roy Webb of Nat West, Rayleigh.

John on crutches, with nephew Ian.

I must say now, that since the loss of my father, Nat West and all the managers in turn, have been very helpful indeed. I met Mr Webb the next day and he was all for buying the farm and immediately made the arrangements for the loan. We bought the farm, but it was a worry to know how we were going to service the loan.

It was a few weeks later when my old friend Fred Ives came into the yard to get some horse food, Fred always had a few horses. We were talking about us buying the farm, the money and one thing and another. In a jokingly way I said to Fred:

"Would you buy that 40 acres at Rawreth and rent it back to me?"

He didn't hesitate:

"Yes OK," he replied. A couple of weeks went by and Fred came in again and commented:

"I thought you were going to sell me that land at Rawreth?"

I told him I did not think he was serious. He told me that Norman had the money there ready for me.. I went over to see Norman and as Fred had said, he was ready to do the deal. The sale of the land helped with the bank loan, and we were able to 'soldier on' more comfortably.

Things were not always plain sailing. One winter in particular we had a very heavy fall of snow and with it strong winds. This blocked all the roads around for miles. Everybody who had tractors, diggers or anything that could shift snow were called in to help. The main problem was to get bread and milk to the elderly and to the outlying dwellings. We ourselves were inundated with phone calls to deliver animal feed; this was because the people who used to collect their feed could not get to us.

We had a large four wheel drive tractor with a ten ton trailer and Dave Fuller (our lorry driver) with Kevin, went out that day three times fully loaded. I think we supplied all our customers and kept them happy. It was about two weeks before all the snow had gone, although the roads were clear;

Page Fifty Seven

Hips, Hay and Harvest

after that things got back to normal, but there was a lot of water about.

Although I did not like these adverse weather conditions, they were always very good for trade. On the feed side of our business, our turnover was well in excess of £8000.00 per week through the winter

We were getting quite a lot of trouble with horse riders riding over growing crops of wheat. They thought because it was green it was grass and that they could ride over it 'willy nilly,' without a thought of the damage they were doing. Also, we had young fellows on motor bikes riding through the wheat and doing a great deal of damage,. You could never be in the right place at the right time to catch them. With all the things that were going on in the farming world and the talk

David Kershaw.

about diversifying, I had a word with my friend Jim Parker.

We discussed about us all getting older and me not being in the best of health, with no descendants to follow on. I had an idea that I would like to turn the farm into a golf coarse. Jim approached a firm with whom he had done business and got them to look into the prospect of getting planning permission. We knew that it would take a lot of money to build the course, club house and other facilities that go with golf courses. We had six acres of land quite close to the building area, and if, and it was a big IF, we were able to obtain planning permission, the land would have raised enough money at that time to have built the whole project.

But I am afraid the planning permission for the building land was a non starter, so we were back to thinking about other ways of going ahead with our plans, although Jim and myself often spoke about it, the project tended to lay dormant.

It was about this time that my Mother was coming up to her 80th birthday and Lilian said she would like to arrange a party for

On mother's 80th birthday Tarzan even left his Jane to come and visit Millie.

Page Fifty Eight

Hips, Hay and Harvest

her. Lilian got in touch with my cousin Betty Goddard, who did catering, and between them they arranged and cooked all the meats, made the cakes, including a birthday cake. Lilian got in touch with all of mother's old friends at her club and invited them all down to the farm.

We had cleaned and swept one of our grain stores out, put bales of straw with planks of wood on for seats and also a lot of chairs and small tables. It turned out to be a wonderful afternoon, sunny and very warm. I think there where about 60 to 70

Mother and myself at her 80th birthday party.

Lilian also hired a 30 seater coach, that used to park at the nursery owned by David Kershaw and was situated opposite the farm. We have been friends of the Kershaw family since they came to live there some years before. Anyway, when the time came for the coach to go and pick the people up, the driver hadn't turned up. We were all at 'sixes and sevens', wondering what to do? David came to the rescue; he said he would drive if I went with him to tell him where to go, bearing in mind that they were spread about in a four and half mile area. We collected them all and they were a happy bunch.

guests there and a good time was had by all. They must have enjoyed themselves because we had a job to get them onto the coach to take them home. Lilian told all the friends that were coming that mother did not want any presents, but if they wanted to give a little money they could do so.

Lilian bought some things for raffle prizes and ran a raffle with the money mother had given to her for her birthday. With the raffle money, mother was able to make a donation of nearly £500 to Southend Hospital cancer research. fund.

Page Fifty Nine

A Time of Worry

It was about a month after her birthday party that mother was taken ill. Our doctor visited her and he said he would like her to be seen by a Mr Ashby, a surgeon at Southend Hospital. He also worked at the Wellesley private hospital. The doctor said we would get an appointment more quickly if we could go privately: we agreed and he rang and got an appointment for the following Friday. It was rather a coincidence that the doctor should suggest Mr Ashby, as we supplied him with corn for his peacocks and pheasants that he and his wife kept as a hobby. Anyway, as we were worried about mother, I rang his home and spoke to Mrs Ashby. She told me that Mr Ashby was away until midday Monday and that I could ring Monday evening. When I rang Monday evening, I apologised for ringing him at home, and explained that we had an appointment with him at the Wellesley on the following Friday, and would it be possible for him to bring it forward at all: he said he could not do this as he was fully booked He went on to ask why I wanted to see him and I told him about my mother's condition. After a brief pause he replied:

"Why wait until Friday, bring her down to Southend Hospital tomorrow morning, be there by eight o'clock and I will see her."

We were there on time and Mr Ashby was true to his word. He examined mother and told her he could not leave her in that state and that he was keeping her in and would operate the following day after he had x-rays done. Mr Ashby phoned us after the 'op' and told us it was a big 'op' and that he had had her on the operating table as long as he dare owing to her age.

He also told us he had put her in intensive care; we went to see her the next day and 'oh dear', she was a poor old thing. The only word she uttered was:
"Lilian."
Lilian gently said:
"Come on Millie you can make it."

We came away after a while with sad hearts, thinking we would not see mother alive again, however, within a couple of days they moved her onto a ward. She was still very ill but still fighting. Mr Ashby had asked to see us to explain the 'op'. He told us what he had done; she had got this collostomy and that she must have been a very strong woman to have come through it so far. Lilian and our friend Sheila went down to the hospital after a few days and did her hair for her: we kept a vigil, going to see her every day. As the days went by mother got stronger and was coming to terms with the things she had to wear.

After a few weeks the hospital matron told us that mother would have to go to a nursing home, or home, if we had the facilities and these was something that we didn't have. Lilian and myself went looking

Mother with grandchildren Simon and Kris.

A Time of Worry

around to find somewhere nice and comfortable. This was a difficult job as all the best homes were full. As a last resort we went to view the 'Ishar Nursing Home' at Stambridge near Rochford. We found the place quite acceptable; there was the choice of two rooms and we picked the one facing east. This was a double room, but if this suited mother, she would be on her own for awhile as they were not too full. Eventually, we moved mother to the Ishar. We still went to see her every day for a couple of hours, as did a lot of our friends, especially Jim and Rene.

They went two or three times a week, so she was never lonely I'm glad to say. Mother was at the Ishar for a few months and got on very well, but I am sorry to say it became very lax and mother became very depressed: we had to do something as soon as possible. Jim rang me within the day, stating that he had heard of a nice home with a vacancy and could we take mother to see if she would like to move there. Jim and Rene met us at Chadwick Lodge, Chadwick Road Westcliff. She liked the place so much that we moved her two days later and she was very happy there.

Our friend Sheila Cater.

The farm and feed business was still going well and required a lot of work to keep things up to scratch. Lilian would go to Rayleigh twice a week, Tuesdays and Fridays

Rene and Jim Parker with Lilian (right) and mother in front.

A Time of Worry

Our friends Jim and Rene Parker.

to bank the takings and do some shopping. While she was away I used to have to be in the office to answer the phone and take orders, then write out the delivery tickets. It was one of these days that a friend of ours came into the office to see me. The lady was Mrs Gina Harold and she had an interest in a golf driving range, along the Hockley High Road. We had the usual chat about one thing and another, and then 'out of the blue', she asked if I would consider selling half of my farm. I asked :

"Why on earth do you want to buy half the farm?"

Terry, her husband, wanted to build a golf course. Anyway, I told Gina I would talk to Terry about it, if he would like to come see me. When Lilian returned from her shopping I told her about the plans for the golf course and we both looked forward to Terry's visit.

Hockley golf driving range.

Page Sixty Two

A New Start

When Terry came to see me, we drove all round the farm and I told him about the investigations we had been having regarding a golf course. The next thing I told him was that if he was interested it would have to be the whole two hundred acres. I explained that I was having a job to make a good living off the two hundred acres now. And I added that through our investigations into having a golf course, we had found out that the planners would only allow the club house and other buildings to be built on the existing site where the farm buildings were situated. Terry went away to give it some thought.

He came back a few days later and we discussed the way he wanted to go. I named my price, he agreed. It was subject to planning permission. At this time I contacted Bob Holland and requested him to work for me in the sale of the farm. The planning permission went on and on, it eventually had to go to the Department of the Environment and that was another long wait, all this time we did not know what to do. Terry did not want us to plant the fields with wheat, so that if the planning went his way, he would be all clear to start constructing the course. In the end I could wait no longer. If he didn't get the permission, I wouldn't have any crops to harvest the next year and then we would be in trouble. So we set to and drilled the majority of the farm with wheat. As it happened, although we were late planting, it all got away and grew well.

If and when we sold the farm, what would we do with the Animal Feed Business? I already had a man lined up who would like to buy the business. It was Mr Victor Pledge, of Stamford Rivers, near Brentwood. He was already in the same business as we were and he wanted to 'spread his wings' into our area. I had been dealing with Victor for quite some time and he had been to see me. We were talking about the hay, straw and feed one day and I asked him if he would like to buy my feed business. He did not hesitate:

"Yes whenever you're ready."

I told him my price, we agreed and did the deal.

Walfords Farm from the air.

A New Start

Now the worrying thing was, if we obtained the planning permission and sold where was Victor going to trade from? It really needed to be somewhere close to Walfords, as all the customers, and there were hundreds of them, found it easy to get to the farm. Then I had an idea and went to see my neighbour, Andrew Pinkerton and told him of my problem. Andrew was very helpful and he said that in the event of Victor having to move, he had a large barn and yard that Victor could rent if it suited him. Victor viewed the barn and yard and agreed it would be all right, but he would sooner stay at Walfords if we did not sell. The following April, we were informed that the Minister had given permission for the Golf Courses, Club House and ancillary buildings, but there was a lot of hassle from the Rochford Council.

Now that things were moving, we had to think about where we were going to move to. We looked around, but could not find anything to suit us. At last we found two old properties in Hullbridge; in fact, these two places were built on part of Hanover Farm that my grandfather sold in 1921, when the Thorpes bought Sheepcotes Farm. We had to clear all the land of the two plots, as they were overgrown by years of neglect, and then demolish the houses. Most of the work of knocking down the houses was done by Arthur Wallaker, a friend and local builder; after all was cleared Arthur built the new chalet for us.

Our new chalet.

Mother was getting a lot stronger by this time; we used to collect her from the home every Sunday and take her out to lunch. After that she would want to go and see the progress of the building of our new house. She was always interested in how it was going. More than once she said:

"Don't have a pokey little old place built, have plenty of room." When it was finished, we ended up with a five-bedroom chalet, mother would come home every Sunday for the day. Lilian always cooked midday on Sunday.

A New Start

Lilian had a bit of a job, because since mother's 'op', she always wanted Lilian to sit and talk to her, so Lilian would sit mother in the kitchen while she cooked the traditional Sunday roast. We also used to pick mother up from the home on Wednesdays and take her to a fish restaurant; 'Bailey's', along Southend seafront. Mother always loved fish and chips and a 'Rossi' ice cream afterwards.

Now that the Golf Course was being built, we had to get Victor moved over to Andrews. By this time most of the hay and straw had been sold so it was only the hard feeds that had to be moved. This was not a hard job, as all of it was on pallets. It was all done by forklift, an easy job for once. The next step was to deal with all the farm machinery and tractors. Bob Holland suggested we put them all into their collective sale. It was being held at Marks Tey, some twenty miles away, towards Colchester and close to the A12. It didn't matter too much about the distance, as we had plenty of trailers to transport everything to the sale ground. Another friend of mine, Johnny MacGirr, who is a car dismantler at Murrels Lane Hockley, came with his lorry and carted a lot of gear to the sale for us.

So what with the tractors and trailers, and John's lorry, we had the job done in about two and half days. All the machinery, trailers, bogies and tractors sold. Well that was the end of another era!

The next problem was all my workshop machinery. I did not want to part with it. Although I was not going to work with it for a living, I did not want to part with old friends; also it had taken me a lot of years to accumulate. Since we had stopped farming, we had been doing some work at Blounts Farm for Norman. I told him of my problem. Again, without hesitation, he said:

"You can have that shed there if it will do you."

I thanked him. David Kershaw and a couple of the lads moved all the gear into the shed. I've been there ever since.

I have still got one tractor, with a loader and bucket, plus a flat eight bale grab. This is also kept at Norman's and it is very handy when Norman has his hay baled. David carts it all into the barn and stacks it with the loader. I like to try and do different jobs for Norman as he has been more than helpful to me. I find it rather difficult to do some things owing to my artificial hips, but we try to do our best.

When we at last left the farm and moved into the new house I had to go up to Norman's each day, as we hadn't built my workshop yet, although we were halfway there. Norman was getting a man to build it for me in sections, so it could be bolted together when we got it onto the site. It was 32ft long by 16ft wide, a nice size shed. I made all the roof trusses myself, made to Henry's measurements, the man who built the shed.

Gina and Terry Harold at Hanover Golf Club.

Page Sixty Five

Turning My Hand to Something New

After the shed was finished I thought I would like to try my hand at wood turning. Bernard found me a second hand 'Harrison Jubilee Lathe' from one of his friends at Horndon on the Hill. I made a start and made a few things, a couple of bowls, light pulls and other odds and ends, not very good, but my new life had begun.

Lilian and I were in Southend one day and as usual I wanted to go to 'Fardon's', the local tool store. We were looking around at all the wood working tools and lathes. As we were going round, we met Mike Frost. I had known Mike for a number of years, he being very keen with the gun and shooting pigeons on our farms, which he had done for the past eight to ten years. We got chatting about one thing and another and he asked what I was doing in the shop. I told him I was going to try my hand at wood turning now I had retired, and I was looking for turning chisels. Going on to explain I was also going to try to get some lessons somewhere. He replied:

"I'm a wood turner and if you would like to come up to my place one day, I'll show you the basics of turning."

Later I rang Mike up to see if it would be convenient to go and see him. I arrived at 'The Chase', Ashingdon, where he lived. Mike and his wife Heather made me welcome then they brought out some of the things that Mike had made. As soon as I saw them I could see that he knew what he was doing when he said he was a wood turner. They were excellent. After a while we went into his workshop, to look at his lathe. After he started it up and explained the workings of the lathe, I could see the great advantage it had over my machine. He told me he had started with one like I had. The difficulty with this small lathe is the changing of the speeds; it's very awkward. Mike went on to say he had seen an advert in a wood working magazine advertising the 'General Lathe', a Canadian built machine. It was fitted with variable speed control. The only trouble was, it cost a lot of money, but because it was the lathe he was looking for he bought it, and has been very pleased with it. So much so, he then persuaded me to buy one.

Jim, Rene, Lilian and myself had decided to take a holiday We went to York for a few days, then on to Harrogate. Someone had said to Jim:

"If you are ever in Harrogate, you must go and have lunch at 'Betty's'."

Anyway, everybody and his uncle were at Harrogate that day, or so it seemed. We parked at the wrong end of town and had to walk back to 'Betty's'. It was all very nice but I hardly think it was worth the trouble. When we got back to the Range Rover, there stood a Traffic Warden, I asked him what was the matter:

"Is this yours?" "Yes," I replied.

"Where is your disc," "What disc?" I enquired.

"The disc you should have bought to park here," the Warden admonished and added "You should read the Highway Code!"

We had never heard of disc parking before, apparently they can be bought in local shops. With that the warden slapped a sixteen pound ticket on the Range Rover and we then drove off towards the Yorkshire Dales still thinking about the Traffic Warden. We said when we

On holiday in the Black Country.

Page Sixty Six

Turning My Hand to Something New

paid the fine we would write a letter, asking them to give the Traffic Warden a pound so his father and mother could get married and with the remaining fifteen pounds send him to a taxidermist and as for reading the Highway Code, when I read the Highway Code in nineteen forty six, there was no mention of parking discs.

near there, I made the suggestion, and it was agreed we go and find the place.

We continued on until we came to the M62. By the map this would take us very close to where we wanted to go. We booked into a Travel Lodge about two miles from our intended destination. After we had

Working at my wood turning lathe.

We continued on and stopped for one night in a hamlet or village where they filmed the James Herriott series. The next day we pressed on heading for Keswick: we stopped in a hotel in Keswick for about five days, visiting most of the lakes. We left the lake district and made for Morecambe, had a quick look round and moved on to Blackpool. We drove right along the coast road and stopped for lunch in a restaurant somewhere along the way. While having lunch, we were deciding where to go next, I looked at the map and saw Warrington, and knowing the firm that sold the 'General Lathe' was situated

freshened up, we drove to Golborne, but when we found the place it was locked up for the night. So we found a pub and had our dinner, deciding to go back in the morning before heading for home. The next morning we rang Mr Cooper and arranged to meet him at his warehouse. After we had breakfast, we met Mr Cooper at his yard. Rene and Lilian went on to look at the shops while Jim and I looked at the lathes: we bought the 'General' and they were to deliver it the following week. Now we had the long ride home as we had come to the end of our break. It poured with rain most of the way and that didn't help a lot, so we stopped a

Page Sixty Seven

Turning My Hand to Something New

couple of times for food, to freshen up and stretch our legs.

The lathe was delivered the following week by Roy Cooper and his son. They got it into the workshop and switched it on to see if everything was working OK. We settled the account and they went on their way as they had to deliver another lathe in Kent. I gave Mike a ring and he came over to give me a start. Following that he came over a couple of times a week to teach me one or two different ways to turn wood. I would think he would agree now that he has had more than a little success.

Mike and his wife Heather travel around to a lot of craft fairs. They have a caravan with an awning and they arrange all the pieces that Mike has made; clocks, barometers, bowls, fruit, light pulls and many other things, all with a professional finish.

Since then, I myself have emulated Mike and made a fair number of simular pieces and sold them to friends of friends with some sold by recommendation. It's a good thing I don't have to make a living at it, or I think I would starve. But I have enjoyed creating the pieces.

Some of the turned pieces I have made.

Page Sixty Eight

More Friends

Since starting to write this story time goes on and I get asked to do all manner of jobs. I mentioned the Cook family earlier on. It is now Mr John Cook and his wife Pauline, who live and work Sheepcotes Farm. John is a great cattle man; he runs a big herd of cows down on Corringham marshes, some two hundred cows. He runs a bull with the cows, or I should say six bulls in the season. These cattle have approximately five hundred and eighty acres to roam over: when the cows have had their calves, the calves run with the cows for a time, then he sells them on for other farmers to fatten for beef. John Cook feeds them in the winter with good straw and hay. The hay and straw used to be baled in large round bales, these were handled with a spike fitted to a front end loader on a tractor.

In 1996, John had the straw and hay baled with the new large square bales; this posed another problem for him. I was having a chat with him one day and he asked if I could make some form of spike, that would be strong enough to pick these bales up, as they weigh anything between seven and twelve cwts apiece. My friend Bernard and I got stuck in and made one of these spikes: we delivered it to

Howie and Minnie Gemmel, getting ready for daughter Janet's wedding.

Sheepcotes Farm and fitted it onto his 'JCB Telliporter'. After John saw how it worked out, he asked us to make another one for his tractor down on the marsh: this we delivered down to Corringham on 12.12.96. As it happened it fitted after a slight alteration. I hoped that both the spikes would give good service.

Loading large bales of straw.

Page Sixty Nine

More Friends

Andrew Gemmel working on the farm.

We had to make another one for Andrew Gemmell, Andrew being the son of Howie Gemmell who has farmed 'New Hockley Farm' for a good number of years, another good friend of mine, since taking over the farm. He was an excellent cattle farmer and milk producer. You would have had to have been a good man, to beat him at his job. But sadly he had a heart attack in 1995, and passed away, a sad loss to the farming community, and all who had the pleasure to have known him. Andrew and his mother Minnie ran the farm together for a while.

William Bird receives a trophy at the Smithfield Show.

Minnie is another 'salt of the earth'. She has worked very hard all the years I have known her. Her main love, I think, is her animals, but she has turned her hand to most jobs on the farm, as well as bringing up her family, two daughters and a son. Both daughters are married, Janet has a home in Yorkshire, on the Whitby moors, Joanna has a home in Lincolnshire, just outside Spalding; her husband comes from the

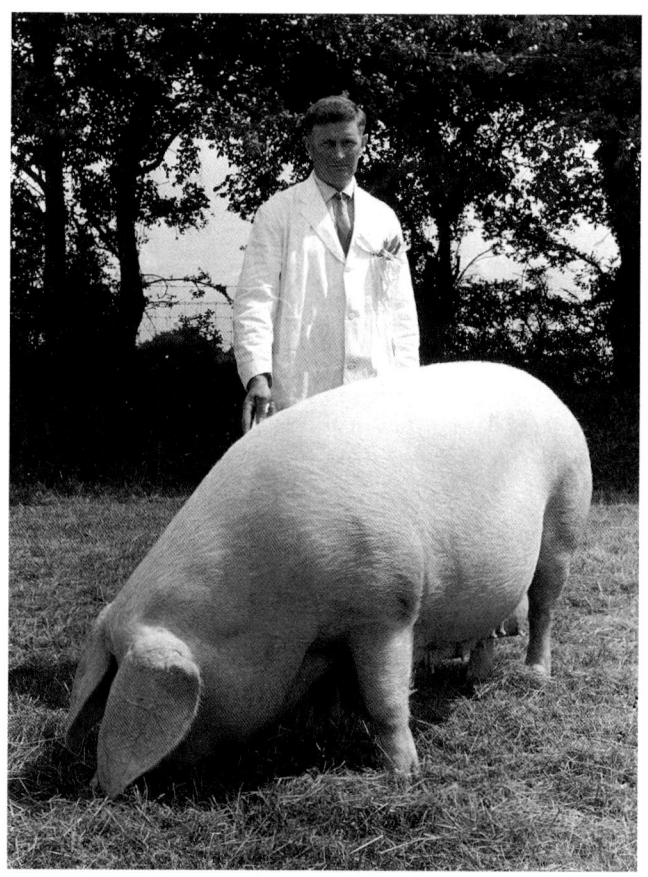

William Bird with one of his prize pigs.

farming world and they all work on the land. I have been told they also grow a lot of flowers. It keeps them all very busy, supplying the various markets, including London.

Andrew, as I have said, stayed at home on the farm with his mother Minnie. After a few years with Andrew, Minnie decided to call it a day and retire. She has now retired to the Whitby moors quite close to her daughter Janet. She is enjoying herself, leaving Andrew to carry on farming by himself. I think he is managing fairly well, although farming is hard going in this day and age.

More Friends

Another farming gentleman who is well worth a mention is William Bird together with his wife. They have farmed 'Wadham Park Farm for a good number of years. Their speciality in the past was 'Landrace Pigs'. William is known all over England for his knowledge of pigs. He has won the top prizes at the Smithfield Shows quite a few times. Now that age is creeping up on us all, William has ceased to keep pigs, but still runs a few sheep, just to stop himself going rusty. William has always been helpful to all and sundry, still drives his cattle lorry, shifting cattle and horses for other people. Well done Willy.

I have mentioned Cracknells Farm earlier, that my cousin Alan Thorpe farmed. He sold Cracknells a few years ago and retired to Devon. A Mr Bolt bought the farm: he was a builder and did not know a lot about farming. What he did do was to pull the old farm house down and build a new modern one, but as I said he didn't know a lot about farming, so eventually he put the farm up for sale. I don't think he had a lot of takers. I was talking to him one day and asked if he was still interested in selling as I knew of a gentleman who might be interested in the farm. The man I was thinking of was Roger Borroughs from Foulness Island. Roger, they tell me was two week's old, when his father Willie, moved to the Island from 'Pinnings Farm', West Hanningfield. That farm is now under a lot of water as the Hanningfield Reservoir was built where the farm originally was. Anyway, I made the introduction and eventually Roger and Ann, his wife, bought Cracknells Farm. They moved there in 1996. So once again, new neighbours. Roger and his son Jason still farm over six hundred acres of land on Foulness, as well as contract farm work for other land owners and also for the MOD on Foulness Island. As far as I can see, whatever job you want done, Roger will tackle it.

I think he will make a great deal of difference to Cracknells Farm. Since writing about Roger and Cracknells there have been more changes. Roger and Sam Stacey had a deal and swapped farms. Sam and Helen moved into Cracknells and semi retired Roger and Ann are now at New Hall, Canewdon. Roger told me he was busier than ever with contract work. Roger has quite a work force who could turn their hands to most jobs. Building barns is one of his ventures, as well as site clearance etc.

Earlier on in this story I have mentioned the Crawfords, that my grandmother worked for. They moved to this area from Scotland and eventually bought 'Fambridge Hall Farm'. They farmed there for a great many years. Their son Jimmie carried on farming the farm after the loss of his father. Mrs Crawford, Jimmie's wife, was a great follower of the Chapel religion and every Sunday she would attend the Hullbridge Chapel that was situated on Ferry Road, opposite Pooles Lane. This Chapel was crushed by a very large elm tree falling across it in a very strong gale. Mrs Crawford worked hard to collect money to build another chapel, running fetes and having small collecting boxes made and given to the villagers to put their donations in. Eventually the new chapel was built on Lower Road, near Coventry Corner. A stone was laid there in her honour, for all the work she had put in to get it built. After the death of her husband Jimmie, Mrs Crawford carried on the farm for a few years, and I think she found it a bit hard on her own. She put the farm up for sale in about 1962, and it was purchased by Henry Gibbon, who also farmed at Great Bentley, near Colchester.

Henry Gibbon had also bought Beckney Farm, Lower Road, Hockley from John Tolhurst about two years before. The two farms make quite a sizable piece of land, I think nine hundred acres in all. The gentleman who is manager of these farms is Mr Tony Mason. He has been with the Gibbon family since about 1965, I myself have known Tony as a friend for a number of years, and have seen him manage the farms with great professionalism.

While I am writing about farmers and farming friends I should mention Roy and Philip Cottis who are father and son farming very successfully. Roy and Philip

More Friends

farm in excess of a thousand acres, their main holding is at Lambourn Hall Farm, Canewdon not to far away is West Hall Farm, Church End Paglesham, this is where Philip lives. The family also farm other farms in the area. Roy, like myself, is of retiring age, but as far as I know Roy still likes to keep his hand in, and carries out his day's work as he has always done. I would think Roy is pleased to have a son to carry on with the farming now, especially with all the EU rules and regulations that have besot the farming world today.

As I drive round different parts of the country and see all the land that has been officially put to 'set aside' it reminds me of how the decline of farming started in the thirties. I once heard Winston Churchill give a speech stating that farming will never again be allowed to fall into decline as it had before the second world war. But I don't think the powers that be today ever heard those comments. It is a sad time for all farmers to see their land growing weeds and the wind spreading the seeds onto other crops, adding another cost to eradicate them. Since I retired from the farming world some ten years ago, I feel I am one of the lucky ones to have been able to get out of all the hassle that farmers and others have to endure in this day and age of the common market. While Roy and Philip can continue farming and fight with all the problems one gets including our weather, I wish them both a lot of luck. As I do, to all those still in farming today.

Memories and Friends, Old and New

I have worked with many farmers over the years. Another I will tell you a little about is Roger Smith. I first knew Roger's father, Mr Alan Smith, another grand old gentleman. I think I'm right in saying that he rented the farm known as Carters Farm, from a Mr Tom Gun, many years ago. This farm was situated in Rawreth Lane. Mr Smith and his family had moved from Burnham Essex, not too far from Maldon, to come to Rawreth. Mr Smith farmed Carters Farm and also another farm near by, known as Blue House Farm, close to the main Chelmsford road at Rawreth. After a few years his son Roger joined him. His father could do with some young blood introduced into his farming, and Roger did just that. After a time with his father, Roger wanted to have a farm of his own and had the chance to take on Stevens Farm at the far end of Bull Lane, Rayleigh. Stevens Farm was farmed and owned by a man by the name of North Gill, a big and rough and ready man, but who got on fairly well with neighbouring farmers. North Gill's life came to a sudden end for he committed suicide. It was said that he shot himself with a twelve bore shotgun, a sad ending for any man.

Roger eventually bought the farm. It was rather run down, but Roger got stuck into it, and after a few years, with a lot of hard work and long hours, got it round almost to his liking. With a lot of hard work as I have said, Roger has made great progress with his farming. He has managed to spread his wings and purchase another farm at Southminster, named Cage Farm, another challenge for him! I think I would be right in saying that Roger has added to the acreage of Cage Farm by buying more land as it has become available. Lilian and I have been to Cage farm when Roger and Eve, his wife, have had a get together with a few of his farmer friends. I must say they both put on a tip top spread. All I can say is:

"Well done Roger and Eve, and good luck to you both."

Another well known character is Rob Warren? He farms with his son at Pickerells Farm together with Boxers Farm, situated between Battlesbridge and Hullbridge along Watery Lane. Watery Lane in the past lived up to its name: most of the winter it would be flooded with about three to four feet of water in places, making it impassable with a motor vehicle. A few years ago the authorities diverted the run of the waterway across the fields, so now it doesn't flood, well only in the most adverse weather conditions.

Rob and his son keep quite a large herd of simmertel animals, mostly for beef. I have known the three generations of the Warren family and a more friendly, helpful family you have yet to meet. Since writing about the Warrens Rob has passed away after a short illness and is sadly missed by all who new him, (a great character).

Further along the same road you come to another farm, Beeches Farm. This has been farmed by the Carter family for a good number of years. When Mr Carter was a younger man he ran a large herd of shorthorn milking cows; he always did his job well. I remember speaking to him in his office one day and he was pleased to show me the stacks of records he had kept for years. All his animals were recorded and he kept these most of his life. Later on, I understand Mr Carter crossed the shorthorn cows with a Hereford Bull, so as to get a good sized beast for beef. I think I would be right in saying that Beeches Farm was of some five to six hundred acres, and like most of the land in this area, is hard to farm, especially when the weather is against you. None the more for that, they made a good job of farming it. One of Mr Carter's daughters, Janet and her husband Michael Jones, were working with Mr Carter for as long as I can remember.

They have both carried on since the passing of the 'Governor'. Michael had the bad luck to have a heart attack in 1996. I am pleased to say he has come through it well and has made a splendid recovery. Good luck Mike!

As I am mentioning a lot of my farmer friends, I must not forget John Robinson. His main base is Canewdon Hall Farm where he lives there with his wife Babs. They

Memories and Friends, Old and New

had three children, two sons and a daughter; Peter, Billy and Sally. Sadly Peter passed away after a prolonged illness, this as you can imagine shattered John and Babs for a very long time; we all felt for them at the time of their loss. But you can't take away the grief of parents. John also farms a lot more land spread around Ashingdon, Rochford, Hockley, Battlesbridge and Bulphan. John, like myself, has had a lot of hip trouble. He had both hips replaced quite a time ago and has had a few more operations on them since, but it doesn't stop him from doing his own thing and succeeding. I have known John and his family for a number of years, and like most farmers they are the salt of the earth, always ready to give a helping hand. Over the many years we have known John and Babs, they have invited Lilian and I out to lunch many times. At their Christmas and New Year get together they included us and always made us very welcome. All I can say is, we are pleased to have the Robinsons as friends!

Another piece about Hullbridge. In about 1950 a family by the name of Trunley bought a house and land from a family by the name of Larner, who were furniture removers in London, quite a large family all boys and hard working. After much discussion they had decided to emigrate to Australia. The sons of Mr and Mrs Trunley, Harold and Vic built a lot of pig styes and went into keeping pigs for a few years. I think I am right in saying that Harold's father was a builder in London, who came to Hullbridge for semi-retirement. They did build the shop now known as Hullbridge Ceramics next to the post office.

After they built the shop, Harold with his wife and brother Vic ran it as an ironmongers and general store for a few years, eventually selling to Terry Shuttlewood. It is still a general store, but Terry's daughter, Lynn has a ceramic studio at the rear. The reason I knew Harold well was that he came and asked if we could cart his large heap of pig muck away. We at that time had two fairly large muck spreaders so were able to do the job for him and spread it onto our fields that were not too far away. We have been friends ever since. We did loose contact for a few years when Harold sold to Terry, but have since met again, in Sainsburys of all places, when I had to go shopping with our daughter-in-law when Lilian had the flu, we have now continued our friendship.

I have mentioned a lot of my friends and the things they do and have done. My old friend Boba Wood for instance. He worked with his father as tree fellers and wood clearance; some of their professional jobs was to take down dangerous trees that were close to houses. After taking the tree down they would put in a charge of explosives to take the root out so it was no more trouble. After Mr Bonker Wood, Boba's father passed away all the boys split up and went their own ways. My friend Boba continued with tree felling and ground clearance in his own right; as his sons got older they joined him in the family business. One of Boba's hobbies was restoring old machines relating to his trade and showing them at the various shows. Uni Powers Timber, Wims Tractors etc.

I have known Boba and his wife Pat for more than fifty years and we have always been friends. Sadly Boba passed away a couple of years ago, greatly missed by all who had the pleasure to have known him.

Lynn at work in ceramics studio.

Page Seventy Four

Memories and Friends, Old and New

I have mentioned earlier in the story about the men whose hobby is vintage agriculture machines. I am friendly with most of them in their 'Rochford 100 Vintage Club'; two of them I have had more to do with than the others. Andy Harland is a friend of mine, Andy, when I first knew him, used to come to Chichester Hall Farm when we farmed there. He would come on a Saturday afternoon with his pieces of angle iron for me to weld for him, he was building a trailer.. The angle iron was mostly from old iron bedsteads that he had collected. He eventually got his trailer made and it was very serviceable. Andy has since made a few more without my help after he got his own welder.

Andy's mate who works with him on restoring machines is Peter Neave, I used to know Peter's father. He was a landscape gardener. The reason we knew him was, we had sold him a few acres of turf. You had to try to raise some money any way you could years ago!

Peter and Andy restore all manner of things; stationary engines, old fashioned implements of all kinds, shape and size and show them at various shows. They are very dedicated to their hobby and it costs them a lot of time and money doing the hobby they like.

Before we go any further I should tell you about Lilian's family. Lilian has two sisters, both married and both younger than her. She did have a brother but he was

Boba Wood with his restored vintage tractor.

killed in an unfortunate accident at work. Lilian has two sons from her first marriage, Keith is the eldest and is married to Lorraine, Keith is a carpenter and maintenance worker for a housing company. Lorraine works at Ashingdon School as a teaching assistant. They have two sons, Simon and Kris. Simon trained as a painter and decorator, passed his exams and now has a good job working for Wallaker Contractors and Builders. We are very pleased for him as he is a very good lad. Kris has not left school yet but is keen to further his education to be a sports teacher. Another good boy and we hope he achieves his goal, at least he is working hard in that direction, at the time of writing.

Barry, Lilian's other son, lives at Rochford with his partner. Barry works for the railway in their offices at Southend. Irene, his partner is what is called a carer, going round helping elderly patients.

Barry has a son and a daughter, Darren is attending college at Colchester while Leann is still at school. Both are doing very well.

Although I am not, they treat me as though I am their real father. If there is anything we want done, it is always done with a good heart. Lorraine calls in on us most days after work to see we are OK and if we want any thing done or got. Lorraine is a very good girl, or I should say woman; although now, every one younger than me is either girl or boy.

Andy Harland and Peter Neave with their restored stationary engine.

Page Seventy Five

Memories and Friends, Old and New

Keith and Lorraine did at one time move to Lincolnshire. They bought a property that had a shop adjacent to the house that sold pottery. Then. with a friend, they opened part of it as a café. This in turn brought in more customers to have a cup of tea or a meal. While they were there they would possibly buy some of the pottery. This worked well for a time, but her friend suddenly told Lorraine she was packing up. She sold what was hers and went. Lorraine couldn't work the café and the pottery, so she closed the café. Then it was the time when everything went rock bottom with the recession and trade went down, until it wasn't worth opening. Lorainne ran the stocks down and closed the shop. She then went to college and trained as a teaching assistant, passed her exams and got a job at the local school, (Well Done 'Tat') Tat is my nick name for her.

After a while, work was getting hard for Keith to find and he had the offer of a good job in the Basildon area and around. They talked it over and Keith asked, if he took the job, could he stay with us during the week and go home weekends.

This was agreed and they put their house up for sale. The property took some time to sell, but eventually they sold to a person who was going to open it as a restaurant (that was where the shop was). Then they bought a chalet bungalow at Hullbridge and moved close to us. A lot better for all concerned!

Soon after their return to Hullbridge they came to visit us one evening, and as families do, we chatted about this and that and they told us of their journey home.

The family, Kris, Lorraine, Keith and Simon.

Memories and Friends, Old and New

Then, later that evening, after Keith and Lorraine had left, I sat relaxing in my armchair thinking about all the changes through life, the main one I think would be the motor car. It was the earlier conversations that brought those thoughts to mind. Of our family moving back down to Hullbridge from Lincolnshire and of the fast comfortable cars of today and of being able to fill up with fuel at most garages on the way down the A1 and M11; both very nice motorways making it a lot easer to get from A to B, Not at all like it was in 1947.

We needed another car and in 1947 new cars were virtually unobtainable and it was a job to find a second-hand car for sale. However, we were offered one and this car came from a director of Fords of Dagenham, it was an Austin 12 1936 model and the cost was £450.00, thinking about it now, that sum was about a week's wages for a lot of people, at the time we bought the car a farm worker's wage was less than three pounds a week. It would have taken around one hundred and sixty weeks wages to pay for it. That is the change round in life.

When my father bought this motor, he did not want to include it in the farm business, and decided to register it in my name, bearing in mind we still had petrol rationing and had to apply to the 'War Ag' for petrol coupons.

Our 'Austin 12' 1936 model.

When father applied for petrol for the other motor he had to list all of the journeys they had made and those he expected to make. This as you can imagine took up quite a few pages of writing and a lot of time. When it came to applying for the new car, father said:

"The car is in your name, so you can get on and put in for the petrol."

I said: "OK but when applying you will help me."

He answered:

"You have been telling me I don't apply for the petrol properly so that is why we never get enough, you're the clever one you do it and see how you get on."

Anyway, mother gave me a few sheets of paper and told me:

"List all the journeys you're going to make."

I then thought I would go and see Bob Withers who was the local taxi man and a friend of ours, he soon filled in the forms and asked how much petrol I wanted, then I told him that we had to list all the journeys we were going to make.

We're not going to do that, he said, I told him how much I thought we would need for the three months, three months being the period you could apply for. He then said:

"Right, we'll double that and put it in, as all business connected with farming."

When I got home and told mother and father what we had done, they said you will get nothing like that total without listing your journeys, so we'll see how clever you've been.

The authorities replied in about a week giving me all the petrol I had asked for, and with a covering letter, saying they hoped I could manage on the amount they had given me. If not I was to reapply and they would help me out. Father 'had the hump' for three days and would not speak to me. After that he was alright, but could never understand how we got all the fuel we wanted.

Page Seventy Seven

More Friends

One of my friends I don't seem to have mentioned is David Stacey. David and his wife Ann have been our friends for many years. David with his two sons John and Richard run a sizable acreage consisting of two farms; 'Scotts Hall Farm', Canewdon and 'Whiteheads Farm', Witham. John is married to Fiona and live in the farmhouse at Witham. John has now taken over the everyday running of the farms. David still keeps his hand in, doing a lot of work on the farms when required, but he is supposed to be semi retired. David has been a very successful and hard working man. His other son Richard, runs the pig side of their farming enterprise. We have been on holiday with David and Ann quite a few times, and always got on very well, David is the sort of man who is always ready to give you a helping hand. (a good mate).

David is also very good at repairing implements and tractors in his workshop. One of his hobbies used to be 'Steam Engines'. He once owned a 'Clayton Shuttleworth' steam engine and he used to show it at steam rallies. He sold the engine a few years ago as it got a bit much travelling round the country with a low loading trailer and unit with a large engine on board. David says he enjoyed it when he was going to the steam rallies.

Since writing this so far I have some more happenings to relate. My friend, Sam Stacey, who is now living at Cracknells Farm, is brother of David Stacey. Sam is also semi retired. As I think I have mentioned before Sam has two Shire Horses. Sam and his wife Helen take these horses to different shows around the country and sometimes to ploughing matches. Also with one of his wagons, he will give rides to children and

David Stacey's restored steam engine.

adults at the shows to collect money for one charity or another: in the past they have used the horse and wagon as a wedding carriage. Sam has quite a few early horse implements and many of these go on show at the 'Barleyland's Steam Rally'. This is one of the biggest rallies to be held in this part of Essex, it is a two-day show that can take all of the two days to see everything. There is something to interest everyone. A wonderful show.

One of the implements in Sam's collection is a 'Smyth Seed Drill'. It was a few months ago that a young lady got in touch with Sam inquiring about the Drill, and made an appointment to call and see him.

They had a long chat. She explained that she was working for ITV and she had got the job of finding most of the props for a

Page Seventy Eight

More Friends

film they were going to make. The film was 'The Mayor of Casterbridge', from the book written by Thomas Hardy. The outcome of her visit was that Sam had agreed to refurbish the drill back to the original condition; as it was about the years 1850-1870, and the drill had to look brand new. Sam asked me if I would give him a hand and this I did. The drill had to be completely taken to pieces so as to paint it properly and a lot of new parts had to be made and fitted, such as the 'tin spouts' that the grain had to run through down to the ground to be planted. As you can imagine, the original tins and chains were rusted through after many years none use. Anyway, I was very lucky to find a man who said he would give it a go. And would be able to make the little tin spouts and connecting chains. and made a first class job of them. Then instead of trying to paint them, I found another firm that did 'powder painting' and the Governor of the firm was more than helpful; another job well done. To paint them in the ordinary way would have been very difficult as they were small tubes. To get enough coulters[1] we had to alter about eight to get a matching set of fourteen. When we had finished and all the drill assembled it certainly looked brand new.

Sam had agreed to take the drill to the place that the film was being made. This was in Wiltshire at a little village called Lacock.

Lacock is a charming village that has been deliberately kept much as it was a century ago. To enter it is like stepping back in time; and of course, this delightful place is a favourite venue with film-makers. Nearby is the exquisite Lacock Abbey where Fox Talbot, in c1840 made the very first negative positive photographs, using a window in the Abbey as his subject. It was Lacock Abbey that the ITV had chosen as their location for filming 'The Mayor of Casterbridge.'

The production team had set-up their props and were filming in the courtyard of the Abbey when we arrived. The Abbey had been arranged to represent an old fashioned market place with the hustle and bustle of the country folk in their mid 19th century attire and this is where the drill was the 'film star'.

Sam and Helen invited Lilian and myself to go down to Wiltshire with them as I had given them help to get the drill in shape. We got the drill loaded up on Sam's trailer on Thursday 21st September 2000, so as to be ready to go on Friday morning. We set off about ten o'clock, and reached our destination about four in the afternoon, the reason it took a long time was that we had two long hold ups on the M4; due to traffic jams. It was a very nice warm sunny day and the weekend was most enjoyable. The drill was filmed on Saturday afternoon. On Sunday morning we loaded up again and headed for home. That's when it started to rain and it kept on raining all the way home. Sometimes the rain was so heavy, one had a job to see the road. When it rained the heaviest, Helen was driving and she did very well; a very good driver.

Remembering another character in the village I recall George Boul. He was one of the best mechanics I have known. George used to work on Canvey Island for quite a large bus company. I think it was owned by a Mr Bridge. This was during the war. George would travel to work on an old motor cycle. As well as his bus work he had his own garage; this was situated where the Budgens store stands now. This site has changed hands several times, I think the people who occupied it longest was the furniture company 'BFW Beautiful Furniture in Wood'. When George had finished his day's work at the bus station, he came home and started work in his garage: he always had a long list of customers as he was such a good mechanic. If he couldn't fix it, I doubt if anyone could.

Our local coalman was always down at the garage getting his lorries repaired. In fact it was quite a meeting place for anyone who had a vehicle that needed a repair, because during the war and for a long time after, you had no choice but to repair as you couldn't get spare parts. George would be

ITV Filming Thomas Hardy's in the Centre Court

The restored drill on a trailer ready for its trip to Lacock.

Lacock Abbey.

The drill on display in the market square.

Dog for sale.

Page Eighty

The Mayor of Casterbridge of Lacock Abbey

Horseman leads horse and drill away from the market place.

The Mayor of Casterbridge.

A stall in the market.

Page Eighty One

More Friends

working until well after midnight and most nights at that, all day Saturdays and Sundays, seven days a week. I used to go down to the garage most evenings when we had finished work. I learned a lot about repairing vehicles and it stood me in good stead all my working life on the farm, especially when farming became more mechanised.

I think I mentioned the time he repaired the cracked block on our tractor. George got married to Nell and they started up a taxi business. They bought two American Lincolns; these cars were nice, streamlined motors. The

After a time George and Nell bought a house and out buildings down by the river opposite the Anchor Public House and adjacent to Anchor Cottages. The house at that time was known as 'Montague House'. The fairly large barn next to the house became George's garage, for his motor repairs. The house was quite large so Nell opened part of the ground floor as a café. At the rear of the house there was another group of buildings. Later, George cleaned them up and re decorated them, turning them into work rooms for Nell. She had a lady's dress making business and she employed about six girls

The Football Team

engines were V12, that means they had twelve cylinders six a side in 'V' form, and used a lot of petrol. George soon converted them to V8, this made quite a difference to petrol consumption. They were painted black and white and really looked smart. They were two of the smartest taxi's about here.

sewing up the dresses which were sold in the local markets. In later years, after George and Nell had sold the property, the house name was changed to 'The Wayfarers'. The new owners still ran it as a café and restaurant for a time. Most of the out buildings have now been pulled down but the place is still open as

Page Eighty Two

More Friends

an Indian Restaurant. I have been told it is very good.

Mr and Mrs Moss, who ran the Anchor Public House for a good many years had a grandson named Ron, Ron had come to live with his grandparents, for what reason I never knew. Ron was the same age as me and we attended school together and were mates at Hullbridge School. Mr Moss was a great pigeon fancier. He had a lot of good birds and was allowed to keep them throughout the war. The reason being his birds were used to carry messages for the War Office. When some of our men were dropped behind enemy lines, they used pigeons to bring back messages. He also got extra petrol, because when a bird returned with a small canister attached to one of its legs, Mr Moss had to get into his car and take it to the Home Office in London.

Mr Alf Moss had a Lancaster motor at that time and it was one of these motors that didn't have a cooling fan. It was all right in the country but as soon as he got into the built up areas of London the motor would boil up. I remember George Boul fitting an electric fan on the car for him. It had a separate switch so as soon as he got into the town he just turned the fan on and it soon cooled the engine and made it safe to continue. Ron had a brother who lived with his parents in London and in the holidays he came down to stay at the Anchor. On one particular holiday when he was here the weather was not all that good.

The Anchor Pub.

As Ron lived at the Anchor and this is right on the edge of the River Crouch, he had his own canoe. Because of the weather, Ron warned his brother not to go out in the canoe, but he did and was drowned. It was another of those great tragedies that seem to happen in life. The parents and grandparents and all concerned were shattered for a very long time. Ron's father took it the worst of all of them.

Another thing that Alf Moss did was to hold the weekly meetings of the 'Buffaloes'. This was held in a club house behind the pub. Alf was also President of the first Hullbridge Football Team for a number of years. After Alf retired as President, my father was asked to take it on. This he did until he passed away and then it was my turn, and as far as I know, I still am.

George Boul's Garage.

Page Eighty Three

Yet More Friends

This is a copy of an article which appeared in a newspaper to promote the sale of plots of land in Hullbridge (c1928)

Three years ago, Hullbridge was a little known village of less than a half a hundred scattered homesteads, approached by an indifferent road, known only to the occasional tourist or the motorist who had lost his way; Hullbridge slept alone, forgotten. Today, a different tale is unfolded, the enterprise and foresight of a few building constructors have unearthed this Essex beauty spot. New homes complete with modern conveniences are rapidly springing up along or near the main road— now a well made and well kept thoroughfare.

Water companies has given Hullbridge baths and modern sanitation, and rival bus companies, seeing the growing needs of the village, compete with each other to provide ample service. Hullbridge is now within easy reach of London or Southend, by bus and train and is as easily accessible as many a London suburb. Its fine ozone-charged air makes it a veritable health resort which may easily rival any of our coastal watering places at some future date. All this present and potential activity is of course reflected in the phenomenal rise in value of land in Hullbridge.

Plots which three years ago were worth £5 are today fetching three or four times that sum, and the incremental movement continues, so that in the course of the next five years a further increase of 100% or more is to be expected.
"Buy now!"

Is therefore the word for you. This is YOUR opportunity, which must be grasped ere some other more farseeing individual robs you of it. A 'gilt edged' investment which cannot depreciate, but which may instead double or treble your capital in a few years. Recently a new factor has appeared, which must inevitably help along the rise. The question of a bridge over the Crouch has become acute for Southend, and it is confidently expected by those most qualified to judge that Hullbridge will be the chosen site. The erection of this bridge will inevitably cause any of the increases prophesied above to be surpassed by a very long way. A few shop sites are to be had by early applicants, get yours now, and gather in the business, which is coming along, even now. Should it not be convenient to visit the estate immediately your opportunity need not be lost on that account. A small deposit will secure an immediate option on any desired plot, subject to it being unsold. You will be met at the station if you write making an appointment. Don't delay. WRITE NOW. To Frank Eddie, Coventry Hill, Hullbridge

Sic.

A Charabanc full of Eastenders visits Hullbridge to view the plots (c1924).
Note the solid tyres. This vehicle had a hood which could be pulled over when necessary.

Yet More Friends

Perhaps Mr and Mrs Withers, who lived in Tooting, saw this article came to Hullbridge and bought a number of plots.

As a consequence I would say that the Withers moved to Hullbridge in the middle twenties. They moved onto the plots they had bought at the top of Coventry Hill on the right hand side: Coventry Hill Service Station now stands on part of the 'plots' once owned by the Withers.

When the Withers first came to Hullbridge I think I am right in saying their business was that of furniture removers. This they had been doing with horses and a pantechnican. This latter was a very large covered wagon, especially those used for furniture removals in those days before motor vehicles came about. It was said that when they moved here to Hullbridge, the wife of Mr Withers senior drove one of these wagons pulled by a pair of horses and loaded with their furniture, goods and chattels. They had driven all the way from Tooting in South London.

A likeable couple, they had four sons and one daughter, Bob, Albert, Les, Gig and Lucy. After they got here the next job for them was to build their house, and this they did. Bart Treganzer, a builder from Rayleigh, built the house for them, and quite a nice house too; it was one of the first chalet type of houses about here. After a few years they got a motorised furniture van. All the boys were very keen on cars. Bob started up a taxi business. Albert drove the lorry and did the removals with the help of his father (Pop as we used to call him).

Gig was the youngest of the family, he also helped his father until he became ill and passed away. Another sad time for the family, especially his mother. It took her a few years to come to terms with loosing her youngest son.

As Bob had more than one taxi, Lucy would do her stint at taking people where they wanted to go, mostly to Rayleigh Station or to Southend. When they hadn't got any removals on, then Albert would take his turn at taxi work. During the war, when some of the families that had had little bungalows built on a plot they had bought in Hullbridge and had been 'bombed out' in London would move down to Hullbridge permanently. Then this was mostly a job for the Withers. When they had arrived at Hullbridge with the furniture and it was winter, the grass roads were too wet and boggy for the lorry to get to their bungalow: then they would hire a horse and cart from my father to take the furniture to the house. This job was done for quite a few years until they got concrete roads. In later years and the war was over, Bob's taxi business was thriving with three or four taxis on the go all the time. I remember he had a large Humber and two Armstrong Siddeleys. These Armstrongs had a fluid flywheel and a 'pre select gear box', you selected the next gear required and then operated the clutch which then changed the gear also. He also had a Buick. All the cars were second hand, but in good condition, as then you still could not buy new motors, as you can today.

Pop Withers was the first man to put in a petrol pump where the garage now stands: this at first was put in for their own use, for the furniture lorries and taxis.

Jack Polly was one of four brothers born in Hullbridge. Jack at one time was a lorry driver for Wiggins, the builders at Thundersley. That was before he met and married Lucy Withers. They had a bungalow built on the hill next to their parents' house, and then Jack took up taxi work.

If my father and mother wanted to go out for a trip in the country on a Sunday evening they would get Jack to take us. We would go to Burnham and Southminster sometimes, or down to Creeksea and have a boat trip on the River Crouch. Les did some taxi work also with an Armstrong Siddeley: he ran his business out of Hockley Railway Station and around that area. In later life he was a coach driver: because Les used to sing, they called him the

Page Eighty Five

The Withers

The Withers' House.

Mrs Withers driving her pony and trap.

Albert with the Armstrong Siddeley.

Bob with the Armstrong Siddeley.

Jack Polly in the Humber taxi.

Jack Polly.

Their first motorised furniture van.

The Buick beside their first petrol pump.

Yet More Friends

singing coach driver. Les joined the army and went into the RASC. He was in the army for a while, and then was invalided out. It was then he took up singing again and he sang at the Kursaal at Southend and at British Legion gatherings. He also performed at the Pavilion, just off Ferry Road to the left along the river front. That place is now known as 'The Smuggler's Den'. Les died at the early age of thirty nine. His wife is still with us in the Village of Hullbridge at the young age of eighty three.

After Pop Withers passed away, his wife was very upset and lonely: although Lucy was close by and went in every day, it didn't help the old lady with her sorrow. Jack and Lucy decided to put their bungalow up for sale and move in with mother. After some time they were able to sell and move in. Jack had a lot of work to do to get all the gardens into shape: he succeeded in the end but it took a long time.

Lucy's mother was a lot happier once they had settled in and lived a contented life until her passing: this, as you might guess, upset Lucy for a long time. Jack was still earning his living at taxiing, he was also taking father on his rounds Tuesdays and Fridays. Jack and Lucy were always our friends, you could say life long friends. There came a time a few years after I had lost my father, when Lucy rang for help as Jack had collapsed at home and she didn't know what to do. I immediately got Lilian in the car and went to see how we could help. As soon as Lilian saw Jack's condition she rang for the ambulance and waited until it came. Then she went in the ambulance with Jack to Rochford Hospital. Jack never really recovered: he got a little better, then had a relapse and passed away. As you can imagine Lucy was in a terrible state. She did have some relatives who came and stopped with her for a time to help. After a time Lucy sold up and bought a small place in Thorpe Bay, next door to a cousin of hers. We still kept in touch with her until she passed away; you could say, "the end of a great friendship."

Albert went into the army roundabout 1940. He went into the 'King's Royal Rifles'. After being in for a time he contracted asthma, and was invalided out, and returned home. To take up lorry driving again with his father in the removal business. They had all sorts of jobs to do in the haulage business when they hadn't got removals to do. One job they had was to ferry land girls to their places of work. It was on one of these journeys that they had an accident with a bus. There was a very thick fog on that particular morning, and they were on their way to Brentwood. The accident happened between Billericay and Brentwood and the whole side was ripped out of the lorry. The girls who were sitting on that side of the lorry were the ones to take the worst of the crash. Two or three of the girls were killed and others injured. Albert was cleared of all blame as he was well on his side of the road.and in those days there were no road markings. However, it unnerved Albert for a very long time and he vowed he would not drive again, but eventually he did.

One happening I have just remembered was when Albert was moving a family from London down to Hullbridge, late in the year 1942, I was aged twelve. The house stood a long way back from Ferry Road, and they could not get the lorry anywhere near the house. Albert came to the farm to get a horse and cart to move the furniture from the lorry to the house: as all the men were out working in the fields, it only left me. We had a pony and cart, so I harnessed up and went down and helped them move. The man they were moving was very particular about his furniture and followed us up and down with each load, but the last time he never came. When we got back to his house with the last load, Albert gave me a bundle of mops and brooms and told me to take them round to the shed. As I got round the back I saw the man lying across the garden. It frightened me so much that I ran round to Albert and said:

"Albert the old chap is lying out flat in the garden." Albert told me to run to Coventry corner and phone for a doctor. The doctor soon came but the poor man was already dead; the wife went into hysterics, I think this frightened

Page Eighty Seven

Yet More Friends

me more than finding the man. It took me a long time to get over the shock of finding someone dead.

Bob was also in the army for quite a time. I can't remember when he came out, but I do remember him having a son, Robert, who eventuality did very well at college. I am told he is now Dr Robert Withers of East Riding College of Teaching in Yorkshire.

The last people to have the shop on Coventry Corner was Mr and Mrs Collis and they ran it as a general grocers and greengrocers' that was in part of the shop. In the other part were sweets, tobacco, ice cream and a small café. This part was run by Winnie, wife of Mr Collis's son Stan. Stan didn't have much to do with the shops; his work was taxis. Through the war years he was given the job of local fireman. They supplied him with a small unit consisting of engine and pump and also a number of hoses. This fire unit he towed behind one of his taxis. There was a funny side to this job. When he was called out to a fire and when he got there, time and again he could not start the 'fire engine'. It was then all rush and tear to get George Boul out to start the engine. This happened one day along Pooles Lane at Mr Caton's yard, long before it became, 'The Tower Caravan Park'. If I remember correctly Mr Caton's business was something to do with peanuts. Anyway, George soon got the engine running and they put the fire out and saved the day.

Because Stan had a fireman's uniform and a peak cap the local lads used to call him 'Captain Collis'

Another character who came to live at Hullbridge a little while after the second world war was Jock Wallace. Jock was known all over the village, especially by anybody who had a boat on the River Crouch. The local children who were old enough went down to the river to play. Jock lived on the river on a house boat. I have been told he would get a few of the local youngsters around him and tell them tales of some of his exploits through the war. Jock served in the 'Argyll and Sutherland Highlanders'; part of his time in the service was spent in the Commandoes. Jock at one time used to ferry people across the river, this was after Dick Hymas retired from the job. He also had a few dinghies. These he would hire out by the hour, about two shillings (10p) per hour. You did not want to be out much longer than that, as they leaked. And you had to bale the water out, that is if you didn't want to sink.

Another thing that happened through the war. The Nursery opposite Walfords Farm was owned by Mr Fred Paish and since moving to the farm we had struck up a friendship with the Paish's and would go down to the Anchor for a drink Wednesday and Saturday evening's. We would get on a bus and it would take us down to the Anchor, the buses used to turn round in the Anchor car park. There was a driver and conductor on the buses at this time, and these two were on duty most of the time on these nights, so we got quite friendly with them. When we got to the Pub and if there was a air raid on, the buses had to stop running, it was when this happened the

Jock Wallace

Yet More Friends

driver and conductor would stop at the pub with us, when the all clear went, we would all go home. The driver was a keen man with a gun, and as the war was on he could not get many cartridges, as we were farmers we had a good allocation. Father used to let him have some so he could go shooting on his time off. It was rather funny really to see the Double Decker bus pull up outside the farm and we all got off. Father would go indoors and get him some cartridges and they would continue their journey back to Southend.

Mr. Moss in his pigeon loft.

Father was very friendly with Mr & Mrs Moss and being farmers we lived a lot better than most, having a big garden and growing a lot of vegetables, also we had a large milking herd of cows and grew many acres of potatoes, kept chickens a few turkeys and pigs, so you see we never went short of food, although we were governed by the Ministries of Agriculture Fisheries and Food and had to be careful of what you did, none the more for that we did help a lot of people out (that was on the QT). We used to let Mrs Moss have some eggs and butter, Grandma and Mother used to make butter all through the war and for a number of years after while we were still on ration. When some of the old chickens had finished laying they would be killed and plucked and put in the pot and boiled with swede carrots and dumplings which made a very good and cheap meal. We also helped Mr Moss out with some corn for his pigeon's (again on the QT). In fact I can tell you now, after sixty years have passed the local constabulary were not behind in coming to get their bits and pieces.

Mr. and Mrs. Moss.

Page Eighty Nine

Ernie the Highler

Another character was Ernie White. Ernie lived with his wife and family in Grasmere Avenue Hullbridge. They had four children, two boys, Bob and Ray. In later years Bob was horseman working for Mr Cecil Hurst at Hylands Farm at the end of Watery Lane. Ray worked for Mr Bon Beckwith at Malyons Farm, Hullbridge. Ray mostly looked after the milking cows. Betty, one of the daughters, passed away at the young age of eighteen. Pam the youngest daughter married Reg Wood, son of Bonker Wood, tree feller and stump blasting contractor. Reg and his sons are still carrying on part of the family business today. (November 2000) Ernie was the local dealer in small animals, and commonly known at the time as 'a higler.' Ernie dealt in creatures such as chickens, ducks, geese, rabbits and many others. Before the war, during the war and for quite a time after, a large percentage of the population of Hullbridge and for that matter all over England, kept a few chickens, ducks, or rabbits. Some even had a few pigs in their back gardens.

People were encouraged by the government to do this during the war so as to provide themselves with a little extra meat and eggs when food was so short and the ration coupons did not allow one to get over fed. The people who kept chickens fed them mostly on the leftovers from meals, plus they could buy small amounts of grain and meal from the local millers. On Monday morning of each week you would see Ernie with his pony and four wheeled trolley loaded up with chicken crates and other boxes for rabbits.

Bob White on a wagon in the winter of 1970.

He would then head off for Wickford Market, as this was held each Monday, with the market at Stamford-le-hope on a Tuesday, Rayleigh on a Wednesday, Rochford on a Thursday, and Chelmsford on a Friday. Ernie's week was very busy.

His customers would have been in touch with him a few days earlier and told him that they wanted to send some of their chickens rabbits or geese to market. Or they may have requested him to purchase some of these animals for themselves. He would do this and bring their money or their purchased animals back when the market had finished. This applied to all the weekly markets. I have known quite a few householders who have kept a pig in the back garden, possibly supplied by Ernie.

He would also take chickens, ducks, and geese to market for my father and mother as mother always had a great number of laying hens: when they had finished their laying period they went to market. Most times they only sold for about two to three shillings each, that is now between 10 and 15p; not a lot of money by today's standard. As I

Bob White ploughing at Hylands Farm.

Ernie the Highler

have said Ernie was a dealer, so when he took our stock to market he would always do a deal with my father for some oats chaff and hay for his ponies. Ernie was kept very busy with his business, especially during the war: he got a lot of different jobs to do, as his horse didn't have to use petrol. Petrol was in very short supply during the war. He also carted lime and manure to all the local allotments, as again during the war householders were encouraged to grow as many vegetables as they could to help with feeding themselves.

Ernie frequented most of the local markets, as at the time I am writing about the markets were a very important feature of country life. They had different places for the various animals. There would be a lot of cows, some bulls, pigs, steers, calves, horses and ponies. Then there would be rows and rows of pens for the chickens, geese, ducks and rabbits. It was always a good day out for the farmers who had something to sell or to buy. It's rather sad that all of this type of market has long gone, in this part of England anyway. I have been told that in some parts of England you can still find some of the old fashioned markets being held, but I shouldn't think there would be many, what with all the rules and regulations we have now since joining the common market.

A 1940's kitchen, note the 'Wireless Set' about half way up on the right with two accumulators to the right of it.

Yet another person I should mention is Barny Louse. He was another character who lived in the village of Hullbridge, off Ferry Road on the corner of Abbey Road and opposite Oakley Avenue. I think it was said that Barny was bred and born in Norfolk. I don't know what Barny did for work, but I do know he used to do a lot of fishing in the Crouch. When we lived at Sheepcotes Farm I remember Barny bringing fish up to sell to my parents, such as cod, skate, eels, winkles, clams, shrimps and the like. The river is very prolific.

I was told he once invented a hair restorer, but as was said at the time, it was not a success. He always had a little old motor car, a 'Singer' I think. I know he was always tinkering with it to keep it running. Barny would also charge up your accumulators to power your 'wireless sets,' we call them radios now, and there were no TVs.

Barny would also come and help father when we were busy at harvest time, stooking the corn or carting to the stack yards, So village and farm life continued then with a largely helpful and interactive community.

Haymaking, Bob White is standing in front and his father Ernie is on top of the hay.

Life and Hullbridge – as it is Now

So far I have only written about 'Paths of former time,' but Hullbridge, although much larger, is still very much a vibrant community which maintains much of its past village atmosphere. But life goes on; and the people of Hullbridge are busy creating 'paths to future time'.

Facilities we have in the village. Perhaps the most important is 'The Riverside Medical Centre' with three doctors, Dr Donnelly, Dr Cornes and Dr Conner, Dr Conner being a lady doctor. These are in my opinion some of the best doctors I have known. Nothing seems to be too much trouble for them to help their patients. And the doctors are also supported with a wonderful group of nurses, as well as reception staff. Again I would say this is one of the finest practices in the country. The practice has been running now for a number of years and is far far better for the people of Hullbridge than it was in years gone by.

To get a doctor then it was necessary to go either to Rayleigh or Hockley. After some years a Dr Bridge held a surgery about three times a week, on the Lower Road; this was in a couple of rooms in a bungalow and it was a great help to the community, but nowhere as excellent as we have with our present Medical Centre.

Maureen Blake, reads the first feature about 'Paths of former time,' in the Evening Echo.

Continuing on with medical matters, we also have one of the best pharmacies that I know, owned and run by Mr Yogesh Patel. Yogesh and his staff are most helpful. Yogesh also collects prescriptions from the doctor's surgery for people who are housebound or elderly, who can't manage to get to the chemist's themselves. He then delivers the medication to their home . I think we are very lucky in our village to have such dedicated people to look after us in our old age. Our grateful thanks to them all.

At the rear of the Medical Centre and situated off of Windermere Avenue, is another very good facility, the 'Day Centre' run mostly by Mrs Babs Port, along with her able committee, with Mr Bernard Timmins as secretary. Anyone over the age of fifty is welcome at the Centre. The Centre supplies hot meals each day. With bingo, pool, dancing, indoor bowls and all sorts of other activities also laid on. This facility helps the people get out rather than looking at four walls all day, and every day. The folk who run the centre do a wonderful job.

The village has a very good library situated on Ferry Road. The chief librarian is Mrs Maureen Blake who has a few very able assistants. This is another great boon for the villagers. They have a photo

Yogesh Patel

Life and Hullbridge – as it is Now

copying facility and a computer and if you book a time you can go and use it; if you want to send Emails you can. And what is more, the staff go out of their way to obtain any particular book you may require. Another great asset to the village.

We now have in the village two fair sized super markets, Budgens at Coventry Corner, the Co-op half way along Ferry Road and both well stocked stores. There is the Golden Crust Bakery next to the Co-op, where you can always get good fresh baked bread, rolls and cakes, six days a week.

Next we have 'Hullbridge Gardening Association' where people can get most of their requirements for the garden, such as seeds, plants and tools.

A little further along Ferry Road we have a Chinese takeaway, and then our local fish shop, quite a good fish and chip shop at that: this shop has been there for many years. It has changed hands a few times, John has been here the longest and now his son has joined him in the business.

Next door to the fish shop is another shop that has just opened as a ladies hairdressers, it is well named, 'Hot Gossip'. The shop has been totally refurbished, and the work was carried out by the girls' husbands. The two girls who now own and run the salon are Deb and Sue. They are well qualified for their job.

Deb and Sue at work.

The building was first built as a garage in 1937 by Mrs Pelling's father, who would put his motor in it and then walk down to the river to do what he had to do, knowing his car was safely in his garage. Later he was asked if he would rent the premises out as a butcher's shop. Seeing what the person wanted, Mr Pelling built two lock up shops in front of the garage, and one was opened as a butchers. This ran for a few years, then Mrs Nell Boul rented the other lock up and opened it selling milk and second-hand clothes. I don't know how long those people lasted in the shops. Later on one lockup was opened by a Mr Chamberlain who used to charge up accumulators that were needed to run a 'wireless'; he also sold bits and pieces for 'wirelesses', such as batteries, valves and I suppose, complete wirelesses as well. Other people took these shops from time to time, one being a Mr Meleir who sold antiques.

In about 1964 Mr and Mrs Pelling opened up part of the shop selling furniture and also in the other part sold saddlery as Mrs Pelling's daughter was into horses at that time.

This lasted for twenty years until 1984, then Mr Pelling was taken ill and sadly passed away. Mrs Pelling has rented the shop out to a number of people in turn trying a few different businesses. Pet foods, florists and such like, but they did not 'take off'. It has changed hands many times since. Up until just recently it was rented by 'Polly Ann's', a florist for a few months. There was not enough trade to give them a living, so they closed. Before them it was a pet food store and green grocery; this also did not last long. It was then opened as a carpet shop, for how long I can't remember, but eventually it closed.

Before Deb and Sue bought the premises from Mrs Pelling they were in a shop on the corner of Pooles Lane. As they had to pass the shop they now have they noticed a 'for sale' sign had been put up. When Lilian, my

Life and Hullbridge – as it is Now

wife, was having her hair done, the girls asked if she knew who the owner was. Lilian said she didn't know; when she came home she asked if I knew the owners. I said I did. I took it on myself to call on Mrs Pelling and to ask her if

Terry Shuttlewood.

she would mind the girls going to talk to her about the possibility of them buying the shop. Mrs Pelling agreed for them to go and see her and eventually they bought the shop. Deb and Sue opened their new salon on the 11th December 2000: we were all invited to the opening, with Mrs Pelling cutting the ribbon for the opening.

The next place you come to is the local Post Office run by Mr and Mrs Livermore. This is another facility in the village run by friendly, helpful people. There was once a post office on its own, in a different building and very small, but none the more for that, very efficient. But that was closed and for a number of years now the post office has been incorporated in the much larger store, next door to the original premises, this being another small super market. This store has also changed hands so many times, it's a job to keep in time with the changes. It has been a Budgens, One Stop, All Days, Dillons: in which order they were, I cannot remember. The Post Office has more room now, and most times it is very busy.

Next to the Post Office is a hardware store owned and run by Mr Terry Shuttlewood and his daughter Lynn. Under the name of 'Hullbridge Ceramics' Lynn makes all the pottery herself, fires it and glazes the finished product. Also, Lynn runs classes, about three times a week, teaching people to decorate the models: one part of the shop has all the finished products on show and for sale.

Terry stocks all the usual things that one wants, most electrical fittings, plumbing, light bulbs, paint and brushes, nuts and bolts, has key cutting service and household appliances are repaired and cleaners serviced. In addition Terry is a computer expert, one of his skills I find very helpful to me; thank you Terry. He has a photo copying service, sends faxes if one requires this facility. Terry is a very knowledgeable fellow on most things electrical and others.

Further along Ferry Road we come to the newsagents, 'Martins' as it is now. I can remember when it was first started, named as 'Launder and Carr Newsagents'. This was Mr Launder and Mrs Carr. It was only a shack of a place then, but they sold and delivered newspapers all round the village, and in all weathers. Then most roads were grass, not a pleasant task, but between them they did the job for a good few years.

Mrs Carr had a daughter with the name of Beattie, who was a dwarf. I suppose her real name was Beatrice, but to everybody in the village she was Beattie, and a nicer person you have yet to meet. Beattie would look after the paper shop when the

June and Derek Livermore.

Life and Hullbridge – as it is Now

others were out delivering. To reach the counter she had to stand on a box, but that did not deter her from doing a good job. Later in life Beattie learnt to ride a bicycle and bought a 'fairy cycle,' as a small child's bike was called then. You would often see her riding about the village and having a cheery smile and a word for everyone. After the paper shop had been sold I remember Beattie getting a job in the Post Office.

Again Beattie stood on a box to reach the counter. Everyone liked her and she handled the post office job very well, she never seemed to let her problem worry her. If she could help someone she would do her best and she joined in everything she could. Children loved her and she loved them in return. I seem to remember she had her cycle stolen at one time, the villagers made 'such a stink' that the cycle was returned. It was never found out who the culprit was. I for one would not have liked to have been in that person's shoes if the villagers had found out who it was.

I think the next man to have the paper shop was a Mr Elliot. The reason I knew this man was because when we had finished our Sunday morning milking and had had breakfast, I would go down to the paper shop to get our paper and some sweets, cigarettes, tobacco and one thing and another. My father always kept a stock of cigarettes for the men who worked on the farm. sometimes in the winter the paper boy who delivered papers to Pevensey Gardens would not turn up. It was then that Mr Elliot got me to do the round for him, an old paper boy at eighteen. After Mr

The ferry crossing, c1920

The River Crouch, where the ferry once plied. AD 2000.

Elliot sold out I believe a Mr Ernie Long took the shop on for a few years. Then I think it went to 'Martins', as it is today.

After the 'Medical Centre' you come to a row of council houses, some of which are privately owned now. These were some of the first council homes to be built in Hullbridge after the war. All of the properties I have mentioned so far are on the left hand side of Ferry Road.

Further along, but on the other side, you come to the school; past the school but back on the left, are a few more shops, an off-licence, a butchers, restaurant, green grocers, sweet shop and another hairdressers then 'All Sorts' a hardware shop and an Indian restaurant.

Just along Pooles Lane on the left there is the 'Community Centre'. This is a very communal place where the villagers can enjoy many leisure activities. At different times of the week, all manner of events are taking place, such as pool, billiards, bowls, dancing, bingo, judo, TAI CHI Chinese Exercises and aerobics. The Woman's Institute meet there, as does the 'Town Woman's Guild', etc. One can always get a cup of tea or coffee at the bar. On Friday and Saturday nights they usually have a small show with someone 'doing a turn,' another good facility for the village.

Another lady we must not forget is Mrs Jackie Tester, Jackie, as she is known by most of the people in Hullbridge. Over

Life and Hullbridge – as it is Now

the years Jackie has got herself involved in most of the events carried out in the village carnival with the children she put a lot of work in, and with great success. Jackie's other labour of love is to run a magazine named ; 'RIPPLES' which she produces about three issues a year. The magazine covers all of the things that happen in the village, such as the doctors surgery times, church service times, together with reports of Hullbridge happenings and reader letters. A real hive of information. Well done Jackie.

Behind the Community Centre is the Anchor pub with its gardens and lawns extending down to the River Crouch close by the site of the old ferry, which as you might expect is at the end of Ferry Road. The gentle river does much to enhance the charm and character of Hullbridge, a name which suggests there was once a bridge here. But that was a long time ago, and for centuries people have crossed the river here by wading or in a horse and cart when the river is low enough or with a rowing boat at other times. Now with so many people owning a car it is easier for them to go to the next village, Battlesbridge, which is well named, and cross the river by road. That leaves Hullbridge with the riverside playground.

There are several yacht clubs along Pooles Lane which extends to the east, namely, 'The Yacht Club;, 'Up River Yacht Club'

The old water tower.

At a summer fair, 2001

and at the far end 'The Brandy Hole Yacht Club'. This name suggests there were once naughty goings-on in Hullbridge. Close by the yacht clubs are two or three caravan sites; one named 'The Tower' for at one time an ancient tower stood on this site, it is now gone

I have come to the end of telling you about Hullbridge and a lot of the characters and happenings as I remember them, some things might not be absolutely correct as memory can play tricks with us all, especially after so many years have passed by. The many people I have mentioned are all real and all who have sadly passed on have all played a part in helping the village of Hullbridge grow and thrive. Although the village has grown out of all recognition from its early beginning it still has a village atmosphere and there are a great many residents who are working very hard to keep Hullbridge as a village.

One thing I must say in conclusion is. If ever there had been a bridge built to cross the River Crouch to Woodham Ferrers it would have been the end of Hullbridge as a village. May the bridge never be built and Hullbridge remain the charming village,it has been for 'donkey's years'.